Christmas
Holiday and
COOKING

by Carol DeMasters

Ideals Publishing Corp.
Nashville, Tennessee

Contents

Director of Publishing: Patricia Pingry
Managing Editor: Marybeth Owens
Cookbook Editor: Cornell M. Brellenthin
Copy Editors: Linda Robinson, Shelly Bowerman
Art Director: Pat McRae
Photographer: Gerald Koser
Food Stylist: Lisa Landers
Typographer: Kim Kaczanowski

ISBN 0-8249-3051-7
Copyright © MCMLXXXV by Ideals Publishing Corporation.
All rights reserved.
Printed and bound in the United States of America.

Published by Ideals Publishing Corporation
Nelson Place, Elm Hill Pike
Nashville, Tennessee

Cover recipes:
Brandy Creme, Apricot Florentines, Secret Kiss Cookies, page 68;
Pumpkin Charlotte, page 56; Fresh Apple and Spice Pecan Bread,
page 48; Candied Pecans, page 70; Rum Cherries, page 72.

Christmas Relish Tree, page 5.

Appetizers and Beverages

Clam Puffs

Makes 2 dozen

1 can (6½ ounces) minced clams,
    drained
2 tablespoons whipping cream
1 package (3 ounces) cream cheese
    with chives, softened
¼ teaspoon dry mustard
½ teaspoon Worcestershire sauce
¼ teaspoon salt
1 teaspoon minced onion
2 tablespoons unsalted butter,
    softened
24 thin slices French bread
    Paprika

Mix clams, whipping cream, cream cheese, mustard, Worcestershire sauce, salt and onion in small bowl. Spread butter thinly over bread slices; then spread with clam mixture. Sprinkle lightly with paprika. Broil until puffy and hot. Serve immediately.

Note: Clam spread can be made at least 1 day in advance and refrigerated. Bring to room temperature before using.

Jalapeno Cheese Ball

Makes 16 to 20 servings

1 pound shredded sharp Cheddar
    cheese
5 whole canned jalapeno peppers
1 large onion, quartered
3 cloves garlic
½ cup mayonnaise
1 cup chopped pecans
    Tortilla chips or crackers

Combine cheese, peppers, onion and garlic in work bowl of food processor fitted with steel blade. Process with 2 or 3 on-off turns to blend. Add mayonnaise; process until smooth. Chill until firm; form into one large ball or 16 to 20 bite-sized balls. Chill. Roll in pecans when cheese is firm. Chill again. Serve with tortilla chips.

Apple Nut Log

Makes one 6-inch log

1 package (8 ounces) cream cheese,
    softened
1 tablespoon apple juice
¼ teaspoon nutmeg
1 teaspoon fresh lemon juice
1 cup chopped apples
1 cup chopped pecans
    Wheat toast or wheat snack
    crackers

Combine cream cheese, apple juice and nutmeg in mixing bowl; blend until smooth. Pour lemon juice over chopped apples. Add apples and ¾ cup of pecans to cheese mixture; blend well. Shape into one 6-inch log and roll in remaining chopped nuts. Wrap in plastic; refrigerate until ready to serve. Serve with wheat toast.

4

Christmas Relish Tree

Makes approximately 8 dozen appetizers

2 bunches curly endive
  Florist picks
1 plastic 9-inch foam cone, about
    1½ feet tall
1 carton cherry tomatoes
1 zucchini, sliced
½ head cauliflower, separated into
    florets
4 carrots, cut into 2-inch sticks
  Radish roses
  Wooden picks
  Chunky Onion Dip

Wash and separate endive; remove tough ends of each leaf. Assemble tree by securing base ends of endive leaves to cone with florist picks. Begin at the bottom and continue to work around and upward, until cone is completely covered with endive. Attach vegetables to endive-covered cone with wooden picks, arranging in pattern to resemble a decorated Christmas tree. Place tree on tray or cake stand and arrange extra vegetables around base, if desired. Serve with Chunky Onion Dip.

Note: To make a radish rose, cut root tip off radish. Cut thin slices from top to-*but not through*-bottom of radish. Leave a little red showing between each slice. Chill in ice water until slices open into a petal-like effect. Drain before serving.

Chunky Onion Dip

Makes 1⅔ cups

1 package (8 ounces) cream
    cheese, softened
⅓ cup chili sauce
3 tablespoons mayonnaise
¼ teaspoon Worcestershire sauce
⅓ cup finely chopped onion
  Fresh parsley

Combine cheese, chili sauce, mayonnaise and Worcestershire sauce. Beat at medium speed of electric mixer until smooth. Stir in onion, blending well. Chill. Garnish with parsley.

Oriental Walnuts

Makes approximately 2 cups

2 tablespoons soy sauce
2 tablespoons Dijon-style mustard
1 tablespoon vegetable oil
1 tablespoon honey
1 teaspoon ginger
¾ teaspoon crushed rosemary
½ teaspoon garlic salt
2 cups walnut halves
½ cup sesame seeds

Combine soy sauce, mustard, oil, honey, ginger, rosemary and garlic salt in bowl. Add walnuts; toss to coat. Drain walnuts and toss with sesame seeds to coat. Place in single layer on lightly greased baking sheet. Bake in 250° oven about 30 minutes, until golden and crisp. Cool. Store in airtight container.

Marinated Shrimp and Artichoke Hearts

Makes 4 dozen

 1 package (10 ounces) frozen
   artichoke hearts
24 medium shrimp
 1 large egg yolk
 ½ cup olive oil
 ½ cup peanut oil
 ¼ cup wine vinegar
 2 tablespoons Dijon-style mustard
 2 tablespoons minced fresh parsley
 2 tablespoons minced fresh chives
 1 tablespoon minced shallots
   Bibb lettuce leaves
   Watercress sprigs

Cook artichoke hearts according to package directions. Drain and refrigerate. Cook shrimp in boiling salted water until just pink. Drain and cool about 10 minutes, until cool enough to handle; peel and devein. Beat egg yolk in medium mixing bowl. Add oils, vinegar and mustard; beat well. Add parsley, chives, shallots, artichoke hearts and shrimp. Stir gently to mix. Marinate 2 hours at room temperature. Drain and serve with wooden picks, or place small portions of drained mixture on bibb lettuce leaves and garnish with watercress sprigs, if desired.

Bacon-Wrapped Scallops

Makes approximately 1½ dozen

 2 tablespoons dry vermouth
1½ pounds large sea scallops,
   halved
 9 slices bacon, halved
 1 can (4½ ounces) whole water
   chestnuts, halved
   Pitted green olives
   Long wooden skewers

Combine vermouth and scallops in bowl; marinate one hour. Preheat broiler. To assemble appetizers, wrap bacon around one piece each of scallops, water chestnuts and green olives; secure on wooden skewer. Repeat with remaining ingredients. Broil 6 to 7 inches from heat source, turning once, until bacon is crisply cooked.

Caviar Pie

Makes one 9-inch pie

 6 hard-boiled eggs, sieved
 ¼ cup unsalted butter, at room
   temperature
 2 packages (8 ounces each) cream
   cheese, softened
   Chopped onion to taste
   Salt to taste
 2 jars (4 ounces each) caviar
   Sour cream

Combine eggs and butter in small bowl; mix well. Press into a 9-inch pie plate. Blend cheese with onion and salt. Turn into pie shell. Spread caviar over cheese mixture. Decorate with sour cream; use a pastry bag fitted with decorative tip, if desired. Serve with crackers.

Frozen Cappuccino, Mock Champagne Punch, Sleigh Ride, page 11;
Christmas Wassail, Hot Spiced Cider, Holiday Creme Eggnog, page
12, Sparkling Fruit Punch, page 13.

Shrimp Dill Dip _____

Makes about 1½ cups

1 package (8 ounces) cream cheese, softened
¼ cup milk
1 can (4½ ounces) small shrimp, chopped
1 teaspoon fresh lemon juice
1 teaspoon Worcestershire sauce
½ teaspoon minced garlic
½ teaspoon salt
¼ teaspoon dried dillweed

Combine cream cheese and milk; beat until smooth. Stir in remaining ingredients. Cover and refrigerate several hours to blend flavors.

Quick Sausage Rollups _____

Makes 2 dozen

1 can (8 ounces) quick crescent dough
2 tablespoons unsalted butter, melted
¼ cup freshly grated Parmesan cheese
1 to 2 teaspoons dried oregano
8 frozen quick-cooking sausage links, thawed

Preheat oven to 350°. Separate dough into 4 rectangles; press perforations to seal. Brush each rectangle with melted butter. Combine cheese and oregano; sprinkle over dough. Cut each rectangle in half to form squares. Place a sausage link on each square; roll up. Cut each roll into 3 pieces; secure each with toothpick. Bake on ungreased baking sheet 12 to 15 minutes, until golden brown.

Indonesian Shrimp in Sambol Sauce _____

Makes 16 to 20 appetizers

1 pound large shrimp in shell (16 to 20 per pound)
1 cup peanut oil
5 cloves garlic, minced
2 tablespoons chopped fresh coriander
2 tablespoons chopped fresh mint
   or 1 tablespoon dried mint
2 tablespoons chopped fresh basil
   or 1 tablespoon dried basil
2 tablespoons crushed red pepper flakes
1 tablespoon turmeric
2 tablespoons rice wine vinegar
1 tablespoon fresh lemon juice

Using kitchen shears, slit shrimp down back; devein, but do not remove shells. Combine remaining ingredients in shallow non-metal casserole. Add shrimp, cover and marinate in refrigerator 8 hours or overnight. Remove shells from shrimp. Baste with marinade and broil about 2 minutes per side. Warm remaining marinade to use as dipping sauce.

Mini Pizza Pastries

Makes 1 dozen

- 1 sheet frozen puff pastry (10 x 15 inches)
- 1 can (6 ounces) tomato paste
- ½ teaspoon dried basil
- ½ teaspoon dried oregano
- 1 clove garlic, minced
  Salt and pepper to taste
- 12 thin slices pepperoni
- 1 fresh mushroom, cut into 12 slices
- 1 to 1½ cups shredded mozzarella cheese

Place puff pastry on cutting board; thaw. Combine tomato paste, basil, oregano, garlic, salt and pepper to taste; set aside. Cut 12 rounds from puff pastry using a 2½-inch cookie cutter. Spread each round with tomato mixture; top with 1 pepperoni slice and 1 mushroom slice. Sprinkle with cheese. Place on lightly greased or nonstick baking sheet. Bake 10 to 15 minutes in preheated 425° oven, until golden and puffed. Serve hot.

Ginger Meatballs

Makes 48 to 60 appetizers

- 1½ pounds ground beef
- 1 large egg, lightly beaten
- 1 teaspoon salt
- ⅛ teaspoon freshly ground black pepper
- 1 clove garlic, minced
- ½ cup finely crushed gingersnap cookies
- ½ cup catsup
- 2 tablespoons light brown sugar
- 1 tablespoon prepared mustard
- ¼ teaspoon ginger

Combine meat, egg, salt, pepper, garlic and gingersnaps; mix well. Form into 1-inch balls and brown in lightly greased skillet; drain. Combine catsup, brown sugar, mustard and ginger; spoon over meatballs. Cover and cook 15 minutes, basting occasionally with juices. Serve immediately with wooden picks.

Note: To make ahead, cook meatballs as directed and cool. Refrigerate several days or package and freeze. To serve, heat in saucepan over medium heat.

Spirited Cheese Spread

Makes 1 cup

- 2 cups finely shredded Cheddar cheese, at room temperature
- 2 tablespoons unsalted butter, softened
- 1 teaspoon prepared mustard
- ½ teaspoon prepared horseradish
- ¼ teaspoon freshly ground white pepper
- ½ cup beer
  Crackers

Combine cheese, butter, mustard, horseradish and pepper in blender. Heat beer until almost boiling; pour over cheese. Blend until smooth. Let stand at room temperature one hour before serving. Serve with crackers.

Sleigh Ride

Makes 4 servings

12 ice cubes
½ cup cranberry juice, chilled
½ cup pineapple juice, chilled
½ cup apple juice, chilled
½ cup gingerale, chilled
2 tablespoons grenadine, chilled
   Sparkling grape juice
4 lime slices

Combine ice cubes, cranberry, pineapple and apple juices, gingerale and grenadine in a cocktail shaker or in a large jar with screw-top lid; shake well. Remove ice cubes; place 2 or 3 in each of 4 tall glasses. Discard remaining ice cubes. Distribute mixture among glasses. Pour sparkling grape juice into each glass and garnish with lime slices. Serve immediately.

Mock Champagne Punch

Makes approximately 9 servings

⅔ cup sugar
⅔ cup water
1 cup grapefruit juice
½ cup orange juice
3 tablespoons grenadine
1 bottle (28 ounces) gingerale, chilled

Combine sugar and water in 1-quart saucepan; stir over medium heat until sugar is dissolved. Boil 10 minutes; cool. Combine sugar syrup, grapefruit and orange juices; chill thoroughly. Before serving, add grenadine and gingerale.

Cranberry Sparkle

Makes approximately 18 servings

4 cups cranberry juice, chilled
2 cups fresh orange juice, chilled
3 bottles (16 ounces each) 7-up, chilled

Combine all ingredients in a punch bowl; mix well. Serve immediately.

Frozen Cappuccino

Makes 4 servings

1 cup prepared espresso coffee, chilled
½ cup whipping cream
12 large scoops vanilla *or* coffee ice cream
4 to 8 ice cubes
   Whipped cream, optional
   Chocolate shavings, optional

Blend coffee, whipping cream, ice cream and ice cubes in blender until slushy. Pour into 4 tall serving glasses. Garnish with whipped cream and a sprinkling of chocolate shavings, if desired.

Apple Nut Log, Jalapeno Cheese Balls, page 4; Oriental Walnuts, page 5; Caviar Pie, Marinated Shrimp and Artichoke Hearts, page 6; Mulled Holiday Punch, page 12.

Holiday Creme Eggnog

Makes 12 servings

- 1 **cup milk**
- 1 **jar (7 ounces) marshmallow creme**
- 6 **large eggs**
- 1 **teaspoon rum extract**
- 1 **teaspoon vanilla extract**
- 3 **cups whipped cream**
  Nutmeg, optional

Gradually beat milk into marshmallow creme until blended. Beat in eggs, one at a time, mixing well after each addition. Stir in extracts; fold in whipped cream. Chill. Mix well and serve in punch bowl. Sprinkle with nutmeg, if desired.

Hot Spiced Cider

Makes 6 servings

- 1 **quart apple cider**
- 8 **whole cloves**
- 1 **large cinnamon stick**
- 1/8 **teaspoon nutmeg**
- 3 **tablespoons fresh lemon juice**
- 6 **lemon slices studded with whole cloves, optional**

Combine cider, cloves, cinnamon stick, nutmeg and lemon juice in 2-quart saucepan over medium-low heat. Cover and heat 30 minutes; strain and serve garnished with clove-studded lemon slices, if desired.

Christmas Wassail

Makes 24 servings

- 1 **gallon apple juice**
- 1 **quart orange juice**
- 2 **cups fresh lemon juice**
- 1 **cup plus 2 tablespoons sugar**
- 1 **can (16 ounces) frozen pineapple juice, thawed**
- 2 **cinnamon sticks**
- 2 **teaspoons whole cloves**

Combine ingredients in large kettle. Bring to a boil; reduce heat and simmer 1 hour. Discard spices and serve hot.

Mulled Holiday Punch

Makes 14 servings

- 1 **can (48 ounces) pineapple-pink grapefruit juice**
- 4 **cups cranberry juice**
- 1 **cup water**
- 1/2 **cup packed light brown sugar**
- 1/8 **teaspoon salt**
- 2 **teaspoons whole cloves**
- 2 **cinnamon sticks, broken in pieces**

Combine pineapple-pink grapefruit juice, cranberry juice, water, brown sugar and salt in 4-quart saucepan. Tie cloves and cinnamon pieces in cheesecloth; add to saucepan. Heat to boiling; reduce heat and simmer 15 to 20 minutes. Discard spices and serve hot.

Sparkling Fruit Punch

Makes 30 servings

 1 cup sugar
 ½ cup water
 2 cans (6 ounces each) frozen
  limeade concentrate, thawed and
  chilled
 1 package (10 ounces) frozen
  strawberries, chopped while
  frozen
 1 quart ice-cold water
 2 bottles (28 ounces each)
  sparkling water, chilled
 1 lime, thinly sliced

Combine sugar and water in 1-quart saucepan; stir over medium heat until sugar dissolves. Boil 3 minutes. Cool thoroughly. Before serving, combine sugar syrup, limeade, strawberries and water in punch bowl. Add sparkling water; float lime slices on top.

Hot Spiced Tea

Makes 4 servings

 4 cups water
 1 cinnamon stick *or* ½ teaspoon
  ground cinnamon
 2 whole cloves *or* ⅛ teaspoon
  ground cloves
  Dash nutmeg
 1 strip (4 inches long) lemon peel
 1 strip (6 inches long) orange peel
 3 or 4 teabags
  Cinnamon sticks *or* candy canes,
  optional

Combine water, cinnamon, cloves, nutmeg, lemon and orange peels in 2-quart saucepan; simmer 5 to 10 minutes. Add teabags and steep to taste. If using ground spices, stir before serving. Serve hot in mugs garnished with cinnamon or candy cane swizzle sticks, if desired.

Mulled Citrus Cider Punch

Makes approximately 26 servings

 1 can (12 ounces) frozen orange
  juice concentrate, thawed
 1 can (12 ounces) frozen apple
  juice concentrate, thawed
 1 can (12 ounces) frozen grapefruit
  juice concentrate, thawed
 2 quarts water
 ½ cup light brown sugar
 2 cinnamon sticks
  Orange slices studded with whole
  cloves, optional

Combine juice concentrates, water, brown sugar and cinnamon sticks in large kettle. Bring to a boil; reduce heat and simmer 10 minutes. Remove cinnamon sticks. Serve hot and garnish with clove-studded orange slices, if desired.

Soups

Elegant Corn Chowder

Makes 6 to 8 servings

- **3** slices bacon, cut crosswise into strips
- **1** medium onion, sliced
- **1** cup diced *or* thinly sliced potato
- **1** can (1 pound) cream-style corn
  Salt and freshly ground white pepper to taste
- **3** cups boiling water
- **1** can (13 ounces) evaporated milk, scalded
- **2** large egg yolks, lightly beaten
- **1** tablespoon unsalted butter
  Chopped fresh parsley *or* chives, optional

Sauté bacon in 3-quart saucepan until almost crisp. Add onion and potato; sauté lightly, but do not brown. Stir in corn, salt and pepper. Add boiling water; cover and cook over low heat about 30 minutes, stirring occasionally. Add milk; continue to cook until very hot. Just before serving, gradually whisk about ½ cup of hot soup into egg yolks. Return to hot soup; stir in butter. Sprinkle with parsley or chives, if desired. Serve immediately.

Hot Holiday Gazpacho

Makes 6 servings

- **1** can (24 ounces) mixed vegetable juice
- **1** cup chopped cucumber
- **½** cup chopped green pepper
- **¼** cup chopped onion
- **1** tablespoon olive oil
- **1** tablespoon red wine vinegar
- **1** small clove garlic
  Croutons

Blend half of all ingredients, except croutons, in blender. Pour into saucepan. Blend remaining half of ingredients and pour into saucepan. Heat, stirring occasionally. Ladle into bowls; garnish with croutons and serve immediately.

Christmas Curried Broccoli Soup

Makes 6 generous servings

- **2** tablespoons unsalted butter
- **1½** cups sliced leeks
- **1** cup broccoli florets
- **1** small clove garlic, minced
- **¼** teaspoon curry powder
- **3** cups chicken stock
- **1** large egg yolk
- **1** cup whipping cream
- **6** small broccoli florets, blanched, optional

Melt butter in 2-quart saucepan over medium heat. Sauté leeks, broccoli, garlic and curry until vegetables are tender. Purée in food processor or blender. Return to saucepan; add stock. Bring to simmer and cook 10 minutes. Blend egg yolk and whipping cream in small bowl. Gradually whisk about ½ cup of hot mixture into whipping cream; return to saucepan. Cook, stirring occasionally, until heated; do not boil. Serve hot, garnished with broccoli florets.

Elegant Corn Chowder, Hot Holiday Gazpacho,
Christmas Curried Broccoli Soup, this page.

Holiday Mushroom Vegetable Soup

Makes 6 to 8 servings

- **2 tablespoons unsalted butter**
- **3 cups sliced fresh mushrooms**
- **1 cup shredded carrot**
- **1 cup thinly sliced celery**
- **1 large tomato, peeled, seeded and chopped**
- **1 medium onion, chopped**
- **1 clove garlic, crushed**
- **1 quart beef stock**
- **2 cups water**
- **½ cup pearl barley**
- **½ teaspoon dried thyme, crushed**
- **½ teaspoon salt**
- **¼ teaspoon freshly ground black pepper**

Melt butter in 3-quart saucepan. Add mushrooms, carrots, celery, tomato, onion and garlic; sauté until tender-crisp. Stir in beef stock, water, barley, thyme, salt and pepper. Simmer, uncovered, about 30 minutes. Serve immediately in hollowed out acorn squash halves, if desired.

Cream of Oyster and Spinach Soup

Makes 6 servings

- **¾ quart oysters**
- **1 pound frozen chopped spinach**
- **3 tablespoons butter**
- **⅓ cup chopped onion**
- **1 stalk celery, chopped**
- **3 tablespoons flour**
- **¼ teaspoon salt**
- **1 small clove garlic, minced**
  Pinch freshly grated nutmeg
- **1 tablespoon Worcestershire sauce**
  Freshly ground black pepper to taste
- **2 cups milk**
- **2 cups half-and-half**
  Whipped cream to garnish

Cook oysters in 1½ cups water until firm; reserve liquid. Purée oysters in food processor or blender. Cook spinach according to package directions. Drain well; purée. Melt butter in 2-quart saucepan; sauté onions and celery until soft, do not brown. Add flour; cook 1 minute, stirring constantly. Gradually whisk in hot oyster liquid; simmer, uncovered, about 30 minutes. Strain. Return to heat; add puréed oysters and spinach, salt, garlic, nutmeg, Worcestershire sauce and pepper to taste. Add milk and half-and-half; simmer over low heat 5 to 10 minutes. Do not boil. Serve topped with whipped cream.

Chevre Soup

Makes 4 servings

- **¼ cup unsalted butter**
- **1 cup shallots, finely chopped**
- **1 quart chicken stock**
- **1 pound chevre, crumbled**
  Chopped chives to garnish

Melt butter in 1-quart saucepan. Sauté shallots until soft, *but not brown*. Add chicken stock; heat, but do not simmer. Add chevre, stirring constantly with whisk, until cheese melts, about 5 minutes. Do not overcook. Garnish with chives and serve immediately.

Rich Potato Soup

Makes 6 servings

   2 tablespoons unsalted butter
 ½ cup chopped onion
   2 cans (16 ounces each) tomatoes
   6 cups diced baking potatoes
 ¼ cup chopped fresh parsley
   1 cup diagonally sliced celery
   2 tablespoons chopped celery
     leaves
1½ cups beef stock
   1 bay leaf
   1 teaspoon salt, or more to taste
 ½ teaspoon dried thyme
 ¼ teaspoon freshly ground black
     pepper
   1 teaspoon fresh lemon juice

Melt butter in 2-quart saucepan over medium heat. Add onion; cook 5 minutes. Add tomatoes, potatoes, parsley, celery, celery leaves, beef stock, bay leaf, salt, thyme, pepper and lemon juice. Bring to boil; reduce heat; simmer 30 minutes or until potatoes are tender. Remove bay leaf before serving.

Corn and Crab Bisque

Makes 6 servings

 ¼ cup unsalted butter
 ¼ cup chopped onion
   2 tablespoons flour
 ½ teaspoon curry powder
   4 cups fresh *or* frozen corn,
     uncooked and puréed
   1 quart milk
   1 cup whipping cream
     Salt and freshly ground white
     pepper to taste
   1 pound cooked crab meat

Melt butter in 2-quart saucepan over medium-high heat. Sauté onions until transparent. Bring to sizzle; add flour all at once. Cook, stirring constantly, about 1 minute. Add curry and corn; cook 5 minutes. Add milk, whipping cream, salt and pepper; bring to a boil. (Recipe can be prepared 3 to 4 hours in advance to this point. Refrigerate; return to boil before serving.) Add crab meat; heat through 5 minutes. Serve immediately.

Stilton Cheese Soup

Makes 6 servings

   2 tablespoons unsalted butter
   1 onion, finely chopped
   5 stalks celery, finely chopped
 ¼ cup flour
 ½ cup dry vermouth
   2 cups chicken stock
 ½ cup milk
 ½ cup whipping cream
   4 ounces Stilton cheese *or* blue
     cheese, crumbled
     Freshly ground white pepper to
     taste

Melt butter in 2-quart saucepan. Add onion and celery; cook until soft, but not brown, about 5 minutes. Add flour; cook, stirring constantly, 1 minute. Whisk in dry vermouth and stock; bring to boil, continuing to stir constantly, until thickened. Simmer over low heat 30 minutes. Purée in food processor or blender; sieve into clean saucepan. Add milk; heat gently. Stir in whipping cream and cheese until melted; do not boil. Season with pepper and serve hot.

Salads

Cranberry Harvest Salad

Makes 16 to 20 servings

5 envelopes unflavored gelatin
¾ cup plus 6 tablespoons sugar
2¾ cups boiling water
1 cup gingerale, chilled
1½ cups ground cranberries
3 cups sour cream
2½ cups lemon sherbet, softened
1½ cups chopped walnuts
    Frosted cranberries, optional

Mix 2 envelopes gelatin and ¾ cup sugar; set aside. Pour 1½ cups boiling water into large mixing bowl; sprinkle gelatin-sugar mixture over water; stir until gelatin is completely dissolved. Stir in gingerale and cranberries. Turn into 10-inch fluted tube pan; chill until partially set.

Combine remaining gelatin and sugar in large mixing bowl. Add remaining water; stir until dissolved. Blend in sour cream and sherbet using electric mixer. Let stand until mixture is slightly thickened, about 5 minutes. Fold in walnuts. Spoon onto cranberry layer in fluted pan. Chill until firm. Line platter with lettuce leaves, unmold salad, and garnish with frosted cranberries, if desired.

Note: To make frosted cranberries, lightly beat 1 egg white until frothy. Moisten cranberries with egg white and roll in granulated sugar.

Pineapple Marshmallow Salad

Makes 12 servings

1 package (3 ounces) lemon-
    flavored gelatin
1 package (3 ounces) orange-
    flavored gelatin
2 cups boiling water
1½ cups cold water
1 can (20 ounces) crushed
    pineapple, juice reserved
2 bananas, diced
1½ to 2 cups miniature marshmallows
2 tablespoons unsalted butter
2 tablespoons flour
½ cup sugar
1 large egg, lightly beaten
1 cup whipping cream
1 to 1½ cups shredded sharp
    Cheddar cheese

Combine gelatins in large mixing bowl; add boiling water; stir until gelatin dissolves. Stir in cold water. Chill until partially set. Add pineapple, bananas and marshmallows. Turn into a 9 x 13-inch glass pan; chill until set. Melt butter in small saucepan until sizzling; add flour all at once. Cook, stirring constantly, about 1 minute. Add sugar, egg and 1 cup of reserved pineapple juice; cook until thickened. Cool. Whip cream until it holds soft peaks; fold into cooled mixture. Spread over gelatin and sprinkle with cheese.

Mandarin Orange Almond Salad with Tarragon Dressing

Makes 6 servings

2 medium heads romaine lettuce, torn into bite-sized pieces
1 can (11 ounces) mandarin oranges, drained
4 scallions, thinly sliced
1 tablespoon finely chopped fresh parsley
   Tarragon Dressing
½ cup slivered almonds, toasted

Just before serving, toss together romaine, oranges, scallions, parsley and Tarragon Dressing. Serve on individual salad plates; sprinkle with toasted almonds.

Tarragon Dressing

Makes ¾ cup

½ cup vegetable oil
¼ cup cider vinegar
1½ teaspoons sugar
1 teaspoon tarragon
½ teaspoon salt
¼ teaspoon freshly ground black pepper
   Dash liquid hot pepper sauce

Whisk together oil, vinegar, sugar, tarragon, salt, pepper and hot sauce until slightly creamy.
Note: Dressing can be made in advance; shake or whisk before serving.

Marinated Mushroom Salad

Makes 8 to 10 servings

¾ cup vegetable oil
½ cup vinegar
¼ cup water
2 teaspoons salt
1 large clove garlic, crushed
¼ teaspoon freshly ground black pepper
1 pound fresh mushrooms, thinly sliced
1½ cups thinly sliced carrot
1 cup diced green pepper
1 medium onion, separated into thin rings
1 can (4 ounces) sliced pimientos, drained
2 teaspoons dry basil

Combine oil, vinegar, water, salt, garlic and pepper in large saucepan. Bring to a boil. Lower heat; cover and simmer 5 minutes. Add mushrooms, carrots, green pepper and onion rings; cover and simmer 3 more minutes. Add pimientos and basil. Chill one day before serving.

Strawberry Coconut Salad

Makes 8 to 10 servings

    2 envelopes unflavored gelatin
    ⅓ cup sugar
      Dash salt
    2 cups milk
    2 large eggs, separated
    1 teaspoon vanilla extract
    ½ teaspoon rum extract
    1 cup flaked coconut
    1 cup whipping cream
    1 pint fresh strawberries, hulled

Combine gelatin, sugar and salt in top of double boiler; set over hot, but not boiling, water. Stir in milk until gelatin is dissolved. Lightly beat egg yolks. Whisk ½ cup of hot mixture into yolks. Return to double boiler; cook, stirring continuously, until mixture thickens and coats back of spoon. Remove from heat; cool. Stir in extracts and coconut. Beat egg whites until stiff, but not dry. Beat whipping cream until it holds soft peaks. Fold egg whites and whipped cream into coconut mixture. Turn into a 6½-cup mold; chill until firm. Unmold on serving platter; garnish with strawberries, and additional flaked coconut, if desired.

Fresh Holiday Fruit with Orange Cream Dressing

Makes 6 to 8 servings

    1 fresh pineapple
    3 ripe pears, sliced
    2 oranges, sliced horizontally
    1 small honeydew melon, sliced
      into spears
    ½ pound red grapes, separated into
      clusters
      Orange Cream Dressing

Remove crown from pineapple; reserve. Cut pineapple in half lengthwise. Remove fruit from shell, core and cut into spears. Center pineapple crown on large round serving tray. Arrange fruit around crown; garnish with grape clusters. Serve with Orange Cream Dressing on side.

Note: All fruit except pears can be prepared in advance, covered with plastic wrap, and refrigerated. Peel and slice pears just before serving to avoid browning.

Orange Cream Dressing

Makes 1 cup

    1 cup sour cream
    2 tablespoons honey
    1 tablespoon freshly squeezed
      orange juice
    ½ teaspoon grated orange rind

Combine sour cream, honey, orange juice and rind; blend well.

Note: Dressing can be made in advance and refrigerated.

Entrées

Beef Rib Roast with Yorkshire Popovers

Makes 12 servings

1 beef standing rib roast, 4 to 6
  pounds
12 Yorkshire Popovers

Preheat oven to 425°. Place roast, fat-side-up, in shallow roasting pan. Do not add water or cover. Insert meat thermometer. Bake 10 minutes; reduce heat to 325°. Roast 22 to 26 minutes per pound for rare meat, 26 to 30 minutes per pound for medium meat, 33 to 35 minutes per pound for well-done meat. (Meat thermometer should register 120° for rare, 140° for medium, 160° for well-done. Roasts continue to cook after removal from oven, so it's best to remove roast when thermometer registers 5° below desired temperature.) Let roast stand 15 minutes before carving. Serve with Yorkshire Popovers.

Yorkshire Popovers

Makes 1 dozen

1½ cups flour
1½ cups milk
 3 large eggs
½ teaspoon salt
   Roast drippings
   Vegetable oil

Combine flour, milk, eggs and salt in a blender container; blend well. Refrigerate 1 hour. Blend again before baking. Combine roast drippings with enough vegetable oil to make ¾ cup. Place 1 tablespoon in each of 12 muffin cups. Heat in 425° oven until hot. Fill each muffin cup half-full with batter. Return to oven; bake about 25 minutes or until golden brown and puffy.

Christmas Apricot-Glazed Ham

Makes 16 to 20 servings

1 boneless ham (8 to 10 pounds),
  fully cooked
1 jar (18 ounces) apricot preserves
1 package (2 ounces) slivered
  almonds
½ cup raisins
2 tablespoons fresh lemon juice
  Whole spiced crab apples,
  optional
  Holly sprigs to garnish, optional

Place ham on rack in shallow roasting pan. Insert meat thermometer into thickest part of ham. Bake in 325° oven 2 to 2½ hours, allowing 15 minutes per pound, or until a meat thermometer registers 135° to 140°. Combine preserves, almonds, raisins and juice in small bowl; mix well. Brush ham with glaze during last 30 minutes of baking. To serve, center ham on serving platter. Garnish with crab apples and holly, if desired.

Beef Rib Roast with Yorkshire Popovers, this page.

Roast Christmas Goose

Makes 8 to 10 servings

1 goose, 8 to 10 pounds, thawed
Salt and freshly ground black
pepper
Stuffing of your choice
(see pages 48-52)

Preheat oven to 400°. Remove neck and giblets from body cavity; remove excess fat from body cavity and neck skin. Pat bird dry with paper towels. Remove wings at second joint or tie flat against body. Rub inside of cavity with salt and pepper. Stuff neck and body cavity loosely. Fasten neck skin to back with skewer. Tie legs together or tuck in back of skin at tail. Place goose, breast-side-up, on rack in roasting pan. Insert meat thermometer deep into thigh muscle; *it should not touch bone.* Roast uncovered 45 to 60 minutes, spooning off fat as it accumulates. Reduce oven to 325°; continue roasting until meat thermometer registers 180°. Stuffing temperature should register about 165°. If thermometer is not available, check for doneness by pressing meaty part of thigh between protected fingers. It should feel very soft. Let stand 15 minutes before carving.

Cold Stuffed Pork Roast

Makes 8 to 10 servings

1 cup finely chopped onion
1 clove garlic, minced
3 strips bacon, finely chopped
Olive *or* vegetable oil
1½ to 2 cups seedless grapes
1 cup chopped fresh mushrooms
1 cup soft bread crumbs
1 large egg, lightly beaten
¼ cup minced fresh parsley
½ teaspoon dried thyme, crushed
¼ teaspoon dried rosemary, crushed
Salt and freshly ground black
pepper to taste
1 boneless pork roast, 2½ to 3
pounds
Grape clusters

Sauté onion, garlic and bacon in 1 tablespoon olive oil until onion is tender and bacon is crisp. Stir in grapes, mushrooms, bread crumbs, egg, parsley, thyme, rosemary, salt and pepper to taste; set aside. Lay pork roast fat-side-down; slice pork horizontally, being careful not to cut all the way through. Open pork to lie flat and spread with grape mixture. Roll up lengthwise; tie with string every 2 inches. Brush with more olive oil; sprinkle with additional thyme and rosemary. Place on rack in roasting pan. Roast, uncovered, in preheated 375° oven 1½ hours or until meat thermometer registers 170°. Cool. Cover and refrigerate. Slice to serve; garnish with grape clusters.

Herbed Rack of Lamb

Makes 6 servings

    2 tablespoons dry vermouth
    ½ cup apple jelly
    2 racks of lamb, 6 ribs each
    6 tablespoons unsalted butter
    1 teaspoon minced garlic
    2 tablespoons minced shallot
  1¼ cups fine bread crumbs
    1 teaspoon dried thyme, crushed
    1 teaspoon dried chervil, crushed
    1 teaspoon salt
    ½ teaspoon freshly ground black
      pepper

Heat oven to 400°. Pour vermouth into a small saucepan; add jelly; melt over low heat. Put lamb on rack in roasting pan; brush with wine mixture, coating liberally. Bake 30 minutes. Melt butter in saucepan over medium heat. Add garlic and shallot; cook just until wilted. Remove from heat; stir in bread crumbs, thyme, chervil, salt and pepper; set aside.

When lamb has cooked 30 minutes, remove from oven. Press herb mixture onto jam-coated meat. Continue to roast until meat thermometer registers 130° to 135° for rare, about 10 minutes. Remove from oven; let stand 20 minutes before carving.

Make-Ahead Party Beef Tenderloin

Makes 8 to 10 servings

    6 tablespoons unsalted butter
    1 clove garlic, crushed
    ¼ pound ground round
    2 medium onions, sliced
    ¼ pound fresh mushrooms, thinly
      sliced
    2 tablespoons chili sauce
    ¼ teaspoon dried marjoram,
      crushed
    ¼ teaspoon dried thyme, crushed
    ¼ teaspoon hickory-smoked salt
    4 drops Tabasco sauce
    2 dashes Worcestershire sauce
    ¾ cup dry red wine
    2 beef bouillon cubes
    1 beef tenderloin, 5 to 6 pounds
      Sliced bacon

Melt butter in 12-inch skillet. When sizzling, add garlic, ground round, onion and mushrooms; sauté until meat loses its pinkness, onions are transparent, and mushroom liquid has evaporated. Add chili sauce, marjoram, thyme, salt, Tabasco sauce, Worcestershire sauce, wine, and bouillon cubes to skillet; bring to a boil. Reduce heat and simmer 20 minutes; remove from heat. Set aside.

Place tenderloin on rack in roasting pan; cover with bacon slices. Broil 8 to 9 minutes; remove bacon. Turn tenderloin and reposition bacon slices over tenderloin; broil 8 to 9 minutes. Discard bacon. Arrange tenderloin in a baking dish; cover with reserved sauce. Refrigerate at least 1 day or up to 2 days.

Preheat oven to 450°. Cover tenderloin and bake 25 minutes or until hot throughout. Remove tenderloin from pan. Strain sauce and juices into sauceboat. Slice tenderloin thinly. Pour some sauce over slices and serve remaining sauce on the side.

Pheasant with Brown Rice Stuffing _____

Makes 6 to 8 servings

- 1 package (12 ounces) brown rice
- 2 chicken bouillon cubes
- ¼ cup unsalted butter
- 3 large celery stalks, chopped
- 2 large onions, chopped
- 1 cup chopped walnuts
- 1 teaspoon sage
- 2 teaspoons salt
- 2 pheasants (about 2½ pounds each)
  Melted unsalted butter
- 6 bacon strips

Prepare rice according to package directions, adding bouillon cubes for extra flavor. Melt butter in 12-inch skillet. Add celery and onion; sauté until tender, stirring occasionally. Remove from heat; stir in walnuts, sage and cooked rice. Rub salt in cavities of birds. Stuff lightly. (Extra stuffing can be baked in covered casserole during last 30 minutes of roasting time.) Brush birds with melted butter; place bacon strips across breasts. Cover and roast in 350° oven about 2 hours, until tender. Let stand 15 minutes before carving.

Turkey Drumsticks with Hot Mustard _____

Makes 4 servings

- 4 turkey drumsticks, patted dry
  Salt
  Cayenne pepper
- 4 cloves garlic, crushed
- 4 tablespoons hot mustard
- 1½ teaspoons dried thyme, crushed
- 2 tablespoons unsalted butter
- 2 tablespoons vegetable oil
- 4 small onions, diced
- 1½ cups dry vermouth
- 2 cups rich chicken stock

Sprinkle drumsticks with salt and cayenne pepper. Mix garlic, mustard and thyme; rub into drumsticks; let stand 1 hour. Heat butter and oil in large skillet over medium heat. Sear drumsticks; remove. Add onion and sauté 2 to 3 minutes. Add vermouth and stock; bring to a boil. Return drumsticks to skillet. Lower heat and cover; bake in preheated 350° oven 30 minutes. Reduce heat to 325°; bake another 60 minutes. Serve immediately.

Cranberry-Orange Cornish Game Hens _____

Makes 4 servings

- 4 game hens, thawed, giblets removed
- ½ cup unsalted butter, melted
  Salt and freshly ground black pepper
- ½ cup whole berry cranberry sauce
- ½ cup orange marmalade
- 3 tablespoons fresh lemon juice
- 1 tablespoon minced onion

Rinse hens; pat dry. Coat inside and out with butter; sprinkle with salt and pepper. Place hens on rack in shallow pan. Roast 15 minutes at 425°; reduce heat to 375° and roast 45 to 60 minutes longer, basting occasionally with drippings. Combine cranberry sauce, marmalade, lemon juice and onion. During last 20 minutes of roasting, brush hens with mixture several times. Brush once again before serving.

Cranberry-Orange Cornish Game Hens, this page.

Cornish Game Hens with Cumberland Sauce

Makes 6 servings

> **6 Cornish game hens, thawed, rinsed, and patted dry**
> **3 tablespoons unsalted butter, melted**
> **¼ cup dry vermouth**
> **¼ cup chicken stock**
> **Cumberland Sauce**

Fold wings back and tie legs together on all hens; place on rack in roasting pan. Brush hens with melted butter. Pour wine and stock into roasting pan. Bake, uncovered, in preheated 375° oven 45 minutes or until juices run clear when thighs are pierced with a fork. Transfer hens to serving platter; untie legs. Spoon a little Cumberland Sauce over hens; serve remaining sauce on the side.

Cumberland Sauce

Makes 1 cup

> **1 large shallot, finely chopped**
> **Rind of 1 orange, cut into julienne strips**
> **Rind of 1 lemon, cut into julienne strips**
> **Pinch ginger**
> **Pinch cayenne pepper**
> **Juice of 1 orange**
> **Juice of ½ lemon**
> **6 tablespoons red currant jelly, melted**
> **5 tablespoons port wine**
> **½ teaspoon dry mustard**
> **2 teaspoons cornstarch**

Parboil shallot 2 minutes; drain. Parboil orange and lemon rinds 5 minutes; drain. Combine shallot, orange and lemon rinds, ginger, cayenne, orange and lemon juices, jelly, wine and mustard. Moisten cornstarch with a little cold water; stir into sauce. Cook, stirring constantly, until mixture comes to boil and is slightly thickened. Serve warm.
Note: Do not include any white membrane in orange and lemon rind strips or sauce will be bitter.

Holiday Leg of Lamb

Makes 8 to 10 servings

> **1 leg of lamb, 6 to 9 pounds**
> **⅓ cup red currant jelly**
> **½ teaspoon grated lemon rind**
> **1 tablespoon fresh lemon juice**
> **¼ teaspoon ginger**
> **½ teaspoon dry mustard**
> **½ teaspoon salt**
> **1¼ teaspoons freshly ground black pepper**

Place lamb on rack in shallow baking pan. Combine jelly, lemon rind and juice, ginger, mustard, salt and pepper in small saucepan. Cook over low heat until jelly is melted and seasonings are blended. Brush lamb with glaze. Roast in preheated 325° oven 20 to 25 minutes per pound, or until meat thermometer registers 130° for rare, 150° for medium or 160° for well-done.

Crown Roast of Lamb

Makes 6 servings

1 **crown roast of lamb, at least 12 ribs**
Salt and freshly ground black pepper
2 **cloves garlic, slivered**

Place lamb on rack in baking pan. Liberally rub inside and outside with salt and freshly ground black pepper. Insert tip of sharp knife into meaty parts of lamb; press garlic slivers deep into slits. Roast lamb in 325° oven for 15 to 20 minutes per pound, or until meat thermometer registers 130° for rare or 150° for medium. (It is not recommended to roast lamb well-done.) Midway through roasting, cover bone tips with paper frills, or aluminum foil. Let stand 15 minutes before carving. *Note*: Serve lamb roast with baked or sautéed fruits or fill center with stuffing of your choice.

Turkey Breast a la Cranberry

Makes 4 to 6 servings

½ **fresh turkey breast, (3 to 5 pounds)**
1 **can (16 ounces) whole berry cranberry sauce**
½ **cup light brown sugar**
¼ **teaspoon cloves**

Rinse turkey and pat dry; place on rack in roasting pan. Bake for 1 hour at 325°. Combine remaining ingredients; spoon enough over turkey to cover. Bake 30 minutes more or until a meat thermometer registers 170°. Let turkey stand 10 minutes before slicing. Heat remaining sauce and serve on the side.

Holiday Stuffed Ham

Makes 18 to 20 servings

1½ **cups finely chopped pecans**
1 **cup fine dry bread crumbs**
1 **cup finely chopped raisins**
¼ **cup chopped candied pineapple**
¼ **cup grated orange rind**
½ **cup honey**
¼ **teaspoon cloves**
¼ **teaspoon ginger**
¼ **teaspoon cinnamon**
¼ **teaspoon freshly grated nutmeg**
1 **cup brandy** *or* **Cognac**
1 **ham (15 to 18 pounds), fully cooked**
Sugar

Combine pecans, crumbs, raisins, pineapple, orange rind, honey, cloves, ginger, cinnamon, nutmeg and enough brandy to moisten, about ⅔ cup. Stuff ham with mixture; tie securely. Wrap tightly in foil. Place on rack in roasting pan; bake 2½ to 3½ hours at 350°. Remove from oven and carefully remove foil. To glaze, sprinkle lightly with sugar. Increase heat to 500° and bake ham 10 minutes longer. Remove from oven and transfer to heatproof platter. Glaze with remaining ⅓ cup brandy. Let ham cool slightly before slicing. Serve hot or at room temperature.

Rice-Stuffed Pork Crown Roast

Makes 8 to 10 servings

1 pork rib roast, 4 to 5 pounds
2½ cups long-grain rice
½ cup wild rice
1 package (4 ounces) dried
  apricots
½ teaspoon cinnamon
½ cup coarsely chopped pecans
½ can (6 ounces) frozen orange
  juice concentrate, thawed
½ cup honey
2 tablespoons unsalted butter
  Fresh orange slices and fresh
  cranberries, optional

Place roast, bone tips up, on rack in shallow baking pan. Insert meat thermometer; it should not touch bone or fat pocket. Cover bone tips with foil. Roast in 325° oven 3½ hours.

Bring 2½ cups of water to a boil in a 1-quart saucepan; add rices. Cover; reduce heat and cook 20 to 30 minutes, until liquid has evaporated. Cook apricots in water about 20 minutes; add cinnamon during last 5 minutes of cooking time. Stir in cooked rice and pecans; mix well. Combine juice concentrate and honey. Fill roast cavity with rice mixture, placing any extra rice in greased shallow baking pan. Dot with butter. Brush roast with orange mixture. Roast meat and rice another 30 to 60 minutes, allowing 35 to 40 minutes per pound, or until meat thermometer registers 165°. Brush occasionally with orange mixture. Transfer to serving platter; garnish with orange slices and cranberries, if desired. Let stand 15 minutes before carving.

Turkey Kiev

Makes 5 servings

¾ cup unsalted butter, softened
2 to 3 sprigs parsley, minced
2 to 3 sprigs fresh chives, minced
2 green onions, chopped
10 thin slices fresh turkey breast,
  patted dry
½ teaspoon salt
  Freshly ground white pepper
1 large egg
1 tablespoon cold water
  Flour
1 cup seasoned bread crumbs
⅓ cup unsalted butter

Combine softened butter, parsley, chives and onions in small mixing bowl; blend thoroughly. Shape into 10 sticks; place on a platter and freeze 20 minutes. Place 1 butter stick on each piece of turkey breast; roll up. Secure with toothpicks. Sprinkle with salt and pepper.

Preheat oven to 400°. Beat egg and water in a shallow dish. Coat turkey with flour; dip in egg mixture and roll in seasoned bread crumbs. Heat butter in large ovenproof skillet over medium heat. Sauté breasts until golden, turning gently with spatula. Place skillet in oven; bake 15 to 20 minutes, until tender. Serve immediately.

Turkey Kiev, this page.

Individual Beef Wellingtons with Wine Sauce

Makes 12 servings

3 pounds beef tenderloin, cut into
12 4-ounce pieces
Salt and freshly ground black
pepper
1 pound fresh mushrooms
2 tablespoons unsalted butter
3 cups rich veal *or* beef stock
1 cup water
6 tablespoons cornstarch
½ cup cold water
½ cup dry red wine
2½ packages (10 ounces each) frozen
puff pastry, thawed
1 egg, beaten, optional

Place tenderloin pieces on a lightly greased pan. Salt and pepper both sides to taste. Roast in preheated 475° oven 5 to 7 minutes; remove immediately; chill. Separate mushroom stems from caps; reserve both. Chop caps; sauté in 1 tablespoon butter until soft and liquid has evaporated; set aside. To make sauce, chop mushroom stems coarsely; sauté in remaining butter until soft. Add stock and water. Bring to a boil; simmer 10 minutes. Thoroughly dissolve cornstarch in cold water. Stir into stock; continue stirring until mixture thickens. Add wine; stir to mix. Cool completely.

Roll pastry to ⅛-inch thickness; cut into 12 squares, 7 x 7 inches. Place 1 tablespoon sauce on each pastry square. Set a piece of tenderloin on sauce; top with 1 rounded tablespoon of sautéed mushroom caps. Drizzle with 1 additional tablespoon of sauce. Moisten edges of pastry with cold water; carefully wrap around beef. Press pastry firmly to seal. Refrigerate 1 hour.

To cook, place pastries on a non-stick baking sheet; bring to room temperature. For a shiny crust, brush pastry with egg before baking, if desired. Bake in preheated 425° oven 15 minutes, until crust is delicately brown. Serve remaining sauce on the side.

Leftovers

Ham and Cheese Strata

Makes 8 to 10 servings

12 slices white bread
12 ounces sliced sharp Cheddar
    cheese
2 cups diced cooked ham
3 tablespoons chopped onion
6 large eggs, lightly beaten
3½ cups milk
½ teaspoon salt (omit if ham is
    exceptionally salty)
1 teaspoon Dijon-style mustard
¼ teaspoon freshly grated nutmeg

Trim crusts from bread, if desired. Cut circles out of bread slices with biscuit cutter; set aside. Place remaining scraps of bread in lightly buttered 9 x 13-inch baking dish; layer with cheese, ham and onion. Arrange bread circles in decorative pattern over top. Beat eggs with milk, salt (if used), mustard and nutmeg; pour over contents of pan. Cover with foil and refrigerate 24 hours or overnight. Uncover and bake in preheated 325° oven 55 minutes. Let stand 10 minutes before serving.

Ham Goulash

Makes 8 servings

2 large potatoes, thinly sliced
½ cup cooked rice
4 carrots, thinly sliced
1½ pounds ground cooked ham
1 green pepper, chopped
1 small onion, finely chopped
2 celery stalks, finely chopped
1 can (29 ounces) tomatoes

Place potato slices on bottom of 3-quart casserole. Top with a layer of rice, then with carrot slices. Sprinkle with ham. Combine green pepper, onion and celery; sprinkle over ham. Cover with tomatoes, slicing through any large pieces of tomato. Cover and bake 2½ hours at 250°.

Savory Ham Loaves

Makes 6 to 8 loaves

1½ pounds ground cooked ham
¾ cup quick-cooking oats
3 large eggs, lightly beaten
2 teaspoons Dijon-style mustard
¼ teaspoon ginger
¾ cup light maple syrup
¾ cup light corn syrup
¼ cup water
2 cups sliced peaches, frozen or
    canned
1 teaspoon fresh lemon juice
⅓ cup raisins
¼ teaspoon ginger

Combine ham, oats, eggs, mustard and ginger; mix well. Shape into 6 or 8 loaves. Place in ungreased 10 x 15-inch jellyroll pan. Bake 30 to 35 minutes at 350° or until heated through. Combine maple syrup, corn syrup and ¼ cup water in a saucepan. Bring to a boil over medium heat. Reduce heat slightly; cook 5 minutes. Toss peaches with lemon juice; add to syrup mixture. Add raisins and ginger; simmer 5 minutes, until heated through. Serve over ham loaves.

Curried Turkey and Ham Croissants

Makes 8 servings

1 pound fresh asparagus, cooked
  and drained *or* 1 package (10
  ounces) frozen asparagus spears,
  cooked and drained
8 thin slices turkey
8 thin slices ham
8 thin slices Swiss cheese
8 croissants, split
  Curry Sauce

Preheat oven to 350°. Arrange asparagus, equal amounts of turkey, ham and cheese on bottom half of each croissant. Place top halves of croissants over cheese. Bake 10 to 15 minutes, until hot. Spoon Curry Sauce over croissants; garnish with paprika, if desired.

Curry Sauce

Makes 1½ cups

¼ cup unsalted butter
2 tablespoons flour
½ teaspoon curry powder
¼ teaspoon salt
1½ cups whipping cream
¼ cup fresh lemon juice

Melt butter in small saucepan. Stir in flour, curry powder and salt. Gradually add whipping cream. Cook, stirring over medium heat, until thickened, about 5 minutes. Remove from heat; stir in lemon juice.

Turkey Tacos

Makes 4 servings

½ cup chopped onion
1 tablespoon vegetable oil
2 cups shredded cooked turkey
1 cup canned enchilada sauce
8 taco shells
1 cup shredded lettuce
½ cup shredded Cheddar cheese
1 small tomato, chopped

Sauté onion in oil until tender, about 5 minutes. Stir in turkey and sauce. Simmer 5 to 10 minutes to heat through. Spoon into taco shells. Top with lettuce, cheese and tomato.

Ground Turkey Hash

Makes 6 servings

1½ cups chopped cooked turkey
3 potatoes, chopped
1 onion, chopped
1 green pepper, chopped
2 tablespoons vegetable oil
½ cup canned tomatoes, drained
½ cup chicken stock
  Salt and freshly ground black
  pepper to taste

Combine turkey, potatoes, onion, and green pepper; blend thoroughly. Heat oil in 12-inch skillet over medium heat; add meat mixture. Cook 10 minutes; add tomatoes, stock, salt and pepper. Cook 30 minutes.

Turkey Tempura

Makes 2 to 3 servings

⅔ cup flour
¼ cup cornstarch
½ teaspoon baking powder
½ teaspoon salt
⅛ teaspoon freshly ground white
   pepper
1 large egg, lightly beaten
⅓ cup milk
   Vegetable oil
1 pound cooked turkey, sliced ¼ to
   ½ inch thick

Combine dry ingredients in bowl. Stir in egg and milk until batter is smooth. Heat oil to 375°. Dip turkey pieces into batter; deep-fry until golden brown and crusty. Serve immediately.

Turkey Salad

Makes 6 to 8 servings

2 pounds cooked turkey meat
1 kosher dill pickle, diced
¼ cup minced green onion
1½ pounds boiled potatoes, diced
½ cup sour cream
½ cup mayonnaise
1½ teaspoons dried dillweed
1 tomato, cut into wedges
1 hard-boiled egg, cut into wedges
6 black olives

Combine turkey, pickle, onion and potatoes with sour cream and mayonnaise. Add 2 teaspoons dill and mix well. Mound on platter or shallow serving bowl. Garnish with tomato, egg and black olives. Sprinkle with remaining dill.

Curried Turkey

Makes 4 servings

¼ cup unsalted butter
1 small onion, finely chopped
1 tart apple, chopped
¼ cup flour
1 to 2 teaspoons curry powder
¾ teaspoon salt
¼ teaspoon ginger
1 cup turkey *or* chicken stock
1 cup milk
3 cups chopped cooked turkey
1 tablespoon fresh lemon juice
3 cups cooked rice
4 slices orange *or* 1 cup seedless
   white grapes

Melt butter in heavy skillet. Add onion and apple; cook until onion is wilted, but not browned. Combine flour, curry powder, salt and ginger; sprinkle over onion and apple; blend. Stir in stock and milk. Heat slowly; *do not burn.* Simmer 5 minutes. Add turkey and lemon juice. Cover and keep hot 5 minutes. Serve on hot rice and garnish with orange slices.

Turkey Cheese Casserole

Makes 6 servings

- 1 **package (8 ounces) medium egg noodles, cooked and drained**
- 1 **package (5 ounces) Boursin cheese**
- 12 **slices cooked turkey**
- ½ **cup unsalted butter**
- 2 **large onions, chopped**
- 1 **clove garlic, crushed**
- 1 **cup dry vermouth**
- 2 **cups half-and-half**
- ½ **teaspoon dried tarragon, crushed**
- 1 **cup dry bread crumbs**

Toss hot noodles with cheese until noodles are coated. Pour into greased 2-quart casserole. Top with turkey slices. Melt butter in skillet; sauté onion and garlic until onion is wilted, but not brown. Pour into blender; add wine. Blend until smooth. Return to saucepan; stir in half-and-half and tarragon. Pour over turkey. Sprinkle with bread crumbs. Bake in preheated 350° oven 35 minutes, until heated through.

Open-Face Turkey Sandwiches

Makes 6 open-face sandwiches

- 6 **slices pumpernickel** *or* **dark rye bread**
- 12 **slices cooked turkey breast**
- 2 **tomatoes, thinly sliced**
- ½ **green pepper, diced**
- 1 **cup mayonnaise**
- ½ **cup grated Parmesan cheese**
- ¼ **teaspoon salt**
- 1 **cup finely diced mushrooms**

Place bread on a baking sheet. Arrange 2 slices turkey and 2 slices tomato on each slice of bread. Sprinkle with green pepper. Combine mayonnaise, cheese and salt in small bowl; stir in mushrooms. Spread generously over sandwiches. Broil until golden brown and bubbly. Serve immediately.

Turkey Pasta Salad

Makes 6 servings

- 2 **cups pasta wheels** *or* **shells**
- ⅛ **teaspoon cayenne pepper**
- ¾ **teaspoon salt**
- 2 **cloves garlic, crushed**
- ¾ **cup French dressing**
- 2½ **cups cooked turkey, julienned**
- ½ **cup diced green** *or* **red pepper**
- 2 **tablespoons sliced green olives**
- 2 **tablespoons sliced black olives**
  Lettuce leaves
- 3 **hard-boiled eggs, cut into wedges**
- 2 **tomatoes, cut into wedges**

Boil pasta in salted water until just tender; drain well. Mix cayenne pepper, salt, garlic and French dressing; toss hot pasta generously with half of mixture. Gently mix in turkey, pepper and olives. Add more dressing to taste. Line serving platter or individual plates with lettuce leaves; mound salad into center of leaves. Garnish with eggs and tomatoes. Pass remaining dressing at table. Serve immediately or refrigerate until serving time.

Accompaniments

Quick Cranberry Sauce

Makes approximately 3 cups

- 1 pound fresh *or* frozen cranberries
- 2 cups sugar
- 1 cup water
- 1/8 teaspoon salt
- 1/4 teaspoon cloves

Combine all ingredients in 2-quart glass casserole. Cover and microwave on high 18 to 20 minutes, stirring every 6 minutes until berries are tender. Serve warm or chilled as relish with meat or poultry.

Cranberry Chutney

Makes 3½ cups

- 1 package (12 ounces) fresh cranberries
- ½ cup fresh orange juice
- ¼ cup cider vinegar
- ¼ cup wine vinegar
- 1/8 teaspoon cloves
- 1/8 teaspoon allspice
- 1/8 teaspoon cinnamon
- ¾ teaspoon chopped fresh ginger
- 1½ teaspoons grated orange rind
- 1 large Delicious apple, chopped
- ¾ cup sugar
- ¼ cup honey
- ¾ cup golden raisins

Mix all ingredients together in large stainless steel pan or kettle. Cook over medium heat; stirring frequently, until mixture thickens. Cool; transfer to covered container and refrigerate. Serve with chicken, turkey or favorite cold roasted meat.

Broccoli Stuffed Tomatoes

Makes 6 servings

- 2 cups small broccoli florets
- 6 small tomatoes
- 2 tablespoons olive oil *or* vegetable oil
- 1 large clove garlic, crushed
- ½ teaspoon dried rosemary leaves, crushed
- ½ teaspoon lemon pepper
- ¼ cup shredded Gruyere *or* Swiss cheese

Bring large kettle of water to a boil; add broccoli florets. Cook 5 to 8 minutes; drain into colander and place under cold running water 1 to 2 minutes. Drain thoroughly. For decorative look, cut thin slice from top of each tomato, then cut a zigzag edge using a sharp knife. Scoop out pulp, leaving a 3/8-inch shell. Heat oil in large skillet; cook garlic 30 seconds over medium heat. Stir in broccoli, rosemary, and lemon pepper; cook until heated through. Fill each tomato cup with broccoli mixture. Sprinkle with cheese. Place tomatoes in small baking pan. Bake in preheated 325° oven 10 to 15 minutes, until heated through.

38

Quick Cranberry Sauce, this page; Frosted Fruit Garnish, page 44.

Orange Sweet Potatoes _____

Makes 6 servings

**3 large sweet potatoes (about 1½
  pounds)**
1 tablespoon unsalted butter
¼ cup fresh orange juice
⅛ teaspoon salt
¼ teaspoon black pepper
¼ teaspoon ginger
3 oranges, chopped

Scrub potatoes; prick with fork. Bake about 1 hour in 400° oven, until tender. Halve potatoes lengthwise and scoop out pulp; reserve potato shells. Mash pulp with butter, orange juice, salt, pepper and ginger. Stir in orange. Divide mixture among 6 potato shells. Bake 15 minutes in 350° oven, until heated through. *Note:* Potatoes can be prepared in advance and refrigerated until serving time. Reheat to serve.

Holiday Stuffed Baked Potatoes_____

Makes 4 servings

4 baking potatoes
1 large egg
¼ cup milk
2 tablespoons unsalted butter
¼ cup finely chopped green pepper
¼ cup finely chopped red pepper *or*
** 1 jar (2 ounces) chopped
  pimientos, drained**
¼ cup minced onion
**1 cup (4 ounces) shredded Cheddar
  cheese**
** Salt to taste**
¼ teaspoon ground white pepper

Scrub potatoes; prick with fork. Bake in preheated 425° oven 55 to 60 minutes, until soft. Remove potatoes; reduce heat to 350°. Cut slice from top of each potato; scoop out pulp without breaking skin. Mash pulp with egg, milk and butter. Stir in remaining ingredients. Spoon into potato skins; place in small baking pan. Bake 25 to 30 minutes, until heated through.
Note: Potatoes can be prepared one day in advance to the point of final baking. Cover baking pan and refrigerate. Bring to room temperature, about 30 minutes, before uncovering and baking as directed above.

Cauliflower Casserole Supreme _____

Makes 6 servings

**1 head cauliflower, broken into
  florets**
¼ cup unsalted butter
**¼ pound fresh mushrooms, thinly
  sliced**
⅓ cup flour
2 cups hot milk
1 teaspoon salt
1 cup shredded Cheddar cheese
2 tablespoons chopped pimiento

Steam cauliflower until tender; drain well; set aside. Melt butter in 2-quart saucepan; add mushrooms and sauté. Blend in flour; sauté 1 minute more. Gradually stir in milk; cook until thickened. Stir in salt, cheese and pimiento. Place cauliflower in greased small, shallow casserole. Cover with sauce; bake 15 minutes in preheated 350° oven.

Deluxe Potatoes

Makes 8 to 10 servings

8 to 10 medium red potatoes, halved
1 package (8 ounces) cream cheese, softened
1 carton (8 ounces) sour cream
½ cup unsalted butter, melted
¼ cup chopped fresh chives
1½ teaspoons salt
Paprika

Boil potatoes in salted water until they can be easily pierced with a sharp knife. Drain; mash and set aside. Beat cream cheese in mixing bowl with electric mixer until smooth. Add potatoes and remaining ingredients except for paprika; beat until combined. Spoon into lightly greased 2-quart glass casserole; sprinkle with paprika. Bake in preheated 350° oven 20 to 30 minutes, until heated through.
Note: Recipe can be made in advance to point of baking. Cover and refrigerate. To serve, remove from refrigerator 15 minutes before baking. Uncover and bake as directed.

Fruit-Filled Acorn Squash

Makes 8 servings

4 small acorn squash, about 3 pounds
¼ cup unsalted butter
½ cup chopped blanched almonds
3 large oranges
1 package (8 ounces) pitted chopped dates
½ teaspoon cinnamon
¼ teaspoon mace

Cut a thin slice from both ends of squash. Cut in half crosswise; remove seeds and stringy portion. Place squash, cut-sides-down, on greased baking sheet. Bake in preheated 400° oven for 35 minutes. Heat butter in small saucepan; add almonds; sauté until golden. Peel and section oranges. Cut each section in half crosswise; reserve juice that accumulates during cutting. Toss orange pieces and juice with almonds, dates, cinnamon and mace. Turn squash; fill with mixture. Bake 10 minutes longer, until squash is tender.

Herbed Vegetables

Makes 6 to 8 servings

6 cups assorted vegetables
¼ cup chicken stock
⅛ teaspoon salt
2 tablespoons finely chopped fresh basil *or* 1 tablespoon dried basil
½ cup finely chopped fresh parsley
½ cup finely chopped scallions *or* green onions

Steam vegetables until tender-crisp. Heat chicken stock in large skillet. Add salt, basil, parsley and scallions; mix. Stir in steamed vegetables. Heat to serving temperature and serve immediately.
Note: Suggested vegetables are carrots, yellow squash, peas, red peppers, broccoli and cauliflower. Cut into bite-sized pieces.

Corn Pudding

Makes 8 to 10 servings

¼ cup unsalted butter
1 cup finely chopped onion
8 large eggs
4 cups whipping cream
2 teaspoons salt
½ to 1 teaspoon freshly grated nutmeg
4 cups fresh *or* frozen corn kernels, cooked

Melt butter in 4-quart saucepan over medium-high heat. Add onion; sauté until wilted. Combine eggs and whipping cream in large bowl; beat lightly. Add salt, nutmeg, corn and sautéed onion; mix well. Pour into 3-quart baking dish; set in a larger pan. Add hot water until it comes up halfway along outside of baking dish. Bake in preheated 325° oven 45 to 50 minutes, until pudding is set. Serve immediately.

Peas and Mushrooms Prosciutto

Makes 4 servings

2 tablespoons unsalted butter
¼ cup prosciutto *or* country-style ham, chopped
3 scallions *or* green onions, thinly sliced
½ pound fresh mushrooms, thinly sliced
1 package (10 ounces) frozen peas, thawed

Melt butter in 1-quart saucepan over medium-high heat; sauté prosciutto and scallions. Add mushrooms; sauté 1 minute. Add peas; sauté until heated through, about 4 minutes.

Pesto Rice

Makes 6 to 8 servings

4 tablespoons fresh basil, chopped
¼ cup freshly grated Parmesan cheese
2 cloves garlic, crushed
3 tablespoons fresh lemon juice
½ cup olive oil *or* vegetable oil
1 jar (2 ounces) sliced pimientos, drained
1½ cups thinly sliced fresh mushrooms
4 cups cold cooked rice
1 green pepper, diced
Salt and freshly ground white pepper
4 or 5 romaine lettuce leaves
Green and red pepper rings

Combine basil, cheese, garlic and lemon juice in blender. While machine is running, slowly add oil. Coarsely chop pimiento; reserve some for garnish. Blend with mushrooms, rice, and green pepper. Add dressing and toss gently. Add seasonings to taste. Cover and chill. Line bowl with lettuce leaves; fill with salad and garnish with pepper rings and reserved pimiento.

Pesto Rice, this page.

Red Cabbage and Chestnuts

Makes 6 servings

1 **small head red cabbage, shredded**
  Boiling water
¼ **cup dry vermouth** *or* **vinegar**
2 **tablespoons unsalted butter**
1 **tablespoon flour**
1 **cup coarsely chopped cooked chestnuts**
1 **cup water**
1½ **tablespoons sugar**
¼ **cup dry vermouth**
¼ **cup raisins**
1 **apple, thinly sliced**

Cover cabbage with boiling water; add vermouth; let soak 15 minutes and drain well. Melt butter in large skillet. Add cabbage; sauté until limp. Sprinkle with flour. In a large saucepan, combine chestnuts, water, sugar, vermouth, raisins and apple; simmer 5 minutes. Add to cabbage and mix well. Cook, stirring constantly, until sauce is slightly thickened and cabbage is cooked, about 4 minutes.

Note: To cook chestnuts, pierce with fork or cut an "X" in the shell. Bake on baking sheet in 400° oven 15 to 20 minutes. Chestnuts are easiest to peel while still warm.

Fresh Cauliflower in Shallot Sauce

Makes 6 servings

1 **head fresh cauliflower, core removed**
1 **teaspoon prepared Dijon-style mustard**
1 **teaspoon salt**
⅛ **teaspoon freshly ground white pepper**
1 **teaspoon powdered sugar**
¼ **teaspoon paprika**
3 **large egg yolks**
¼ **cup vegetable oil**
1 **teaspoon tarragon vinegar**
1½ **teaspoons minced shallots**
2 **tablespoons unsalted butter**
1½ **teaspoons minced fresh parsley**

Steam cauliflower until tender; keep warm. Combine mustard, salt, pepper, sugar, paprika, egg yolks, oil, vinegar, and shallots in top of double boiler over hot water. Cook, stirring constantly, until thickened. Remove from heat; beat in butter and parsley. Pour over warm cauliflower; serve immediately.

Frosted Fruit Garnish

Makes 1½ pounds

1 **pound green seedless grapes**
1 **large egg white, beaten until frothy**
  Granulated sugar
½ **pound cranberries**

Break grapes into small clusters. Dip into beaten egg white; let excess drip off. Dip fruit in sugar to coat. Place on rack to dry 2 hours. Repeat with cranberries. Use to decorate meat platters.

Breads and Stuffings

Cranberry Scones

Makes 6 large scones

   3 cups flour
   ¼ cup plus ⅓ cup sugar
   4 teaspoons baking powder
   ½ teaspoon baking soda
   ½ teaspoon salt
   ½ cup unsalted butter
   ¾ cup fresh cranberries
   1 teaspoon grated orange rind
   ⅔ cup buttermilk
   1 large egg

Combine flour, ¼ cup sugar, baking powder, baking soda and salt in large mixing bowl. Cut in butter until coarse crumbs are formed. Combine cranberries, ⅓ cup sugar and rind in small bowl; stir into flour mixture. Combine buttermilk and egg; stir into dry ingredients until moistened. If dough is too moist to form into a ball, sprinkle with additional flour. Knead on floured surface 5 or 6 times, until dough is mixed. Cut into 6 pieces; shape into balls. Place on greased baking sheet. Bake in preheated 375° oven 25 to 30 minutes, until golden brown. Brush with soft butter and serve warm.

Sugar Plum Muffins and Lemon Glaze

Makes 1 dozen

   1 cup sugar
   2 large eggs, lightly beaten
   ½ teaspoon vanilla
   ½ cup vegetable oil
   1 jar (7¾ ounces) baby food plums
   1 cup flour
   ½ teaspoon baking powder
   ¼ teaspoon cinnamon
   ¼ teaspoon cloves
   Lemon Glaze

Beat sugar, eggs, vanilla, oil and plums in large mixing bowl. Add flour, baking powder, cinnamon and cloves; blend well. Fill 12 lightly greased muffin cups two-thirds full. Bake in preheated 400° oven for 15 to 20 minutes. While still hot, spoon Lemon Glaze over muffins.

Lemon Glaze

Makes ½ cup

   ½ cup powdered sugar
   1 tablespoon unsalted butter, softened
   1 tablespoon fresh lemon juice

Combine powdered sugar, butter and lemon juice in small mixing bowl; stir until blended.

45

Banana-Apricot Nut Bread

Makes 1 loaf

- 1 cup flour
- 1 cup whole wheat flour
- 1 teaspoon baking powder
- ½ teaspoon baking soda
- ½ teaspoon salt
- 1 cup sugar
- ½ cup chopped dried apricots
- ½ cup chopped walnuts
- ¾ cup mashed ripe banana
- ½ cup milk
- 1 large egg
- ¼ cup unsalted butter, melted

Preheat oven to 350°. Combine flours, baking powder, baking soda, salt and sugar in large mixing bowl; blend. Add apricots and nuts; mix thoroughly. Combine banana, milk, egg and butter in separate bowl; stir just until combined. Add to dry ingredients; mix well. Pour into greased 8 x 4 x 2-inch loaf pan. Bake 1 hour 15 minutes, or until bread begins to pull away from sides of pan and toothpick inserted in center comes out clean. Cool in pan 10 minutes; turn out onto rack and cool completely.

Christmas Pear Bread

Makes 1 loaf

- 1¼ cups corn oil
- 3 large eggs, well beaten
- 2 teaspoons vanilla
- 2 cups sugar
- 1 teaspoon baking soda
- 1 teaspoon cinnamon
- ½ teaspoon salt
- 3 cups flour
- 1 cup chopped pecans
- 3 cups chopped pears
- 1 tablespoon fresh lemon juice

Combine oil, eggs, vanilla and sugar; mix well. Combine dry ingredients; add to sugar mixture; reserve ¼ cup. Mix well. Sprinkle pears with lemon juice; combine with nuts and coat with remaining dry ingredients. Mix into batter. Pour into greased 9 x 5 x 3-inch loaf pan; bake in preheated 350° oven 1 hour.

Festive Holiday Bread

Makes 2 loaves

- ¾ cup light brown sugar
- ½ cup unsalted butter
- 2 large eggs
- 3 ripe bananas, sliced
- 2 cups flour
- 1 teaspoon baking soda
- 1 teaspoon baking powder
- ¾ cup chopped nuts
- ½ cup semisweet chocolate chips
- ⅓ cup finely chopped pitted dates
- ⅓ cup chopped maraschino cherries

Cream sugar and butter in large mixing bowl until fluffy. Beat in eggs and bananas. Add flour, baking soda and powder; mix just until blended. Stir in nuts, chocolate chips, dates and cherries. Pour into two 8 x 4 x 2-inch loaf pans; bake in preheated 350° oven 30 to 40 minutes, or until wooden pick inserted in center comes out clean. Cool and wrap; let stand overnight before slicing.

Festive Holiday Bread, this page.

Fresh Apple and Spice Pecan Bread

Makes 1 loaf

½ cup unsalted butter
1¼ cups light brown sugar
2 large eggs
3 tablespoons sour cream
2 cups finely chopped tart apples
2 cups flour
2 teaspoons baking powder
1 teaspoon baking soda
1 teaspoon salt
½ teaspoon ginger
½ teaspoon cinnamon
½ teaspoon freshly grated nutmeg
1½ cups chopped pecans
Honey

Preheat oven to 350°. Grease and line a 9 x 5 x 2-inch loaf pan with waxed paper; set aside. Cream butter in large mixing bowl. Add brown sugar; mix until fluffy. Add eggs, 1 at a time; continue beating 1 to 2 minutes. Stir in sour cream and apples. Sift flour, baking powder, baking soda, salt, ginger, cinnamon and nutmeg together into another bowl. Mix in 1 cup nuts. Mix into apple batter. Pour into pan; smooth top. Let rest 20 minutes. Bake 60 to 75 minutes or until toothpick inserted in center comes out clean. Cool 15 minutes in pan. Glaze top of bread lightly with honey; top with remaining nuts.

Cranberry Bread

Makes 1 loaf

2 cups flour
1 cup sugar
1½ tablespoons baking powder
½ teaspoon baking soda
1 teaspoon salt
¼ cup unsalted butter
¾ cup fresh orange juice
1 tablespoon grated orange rind
1 large egg, lightly beaten
1 cup chopped nuts
2 cups fresh *or* frozen cranberries, coarsely chopped

Sift flour, sugar, baking powder, baking soda and salt into a large bowl. Cut in butter until mixture resembles coarse cornmeal. Combine orange juice and rind with egg; pour all at once into dry ingredients. Mix to dampen flour. Gently fold in nuts and cranberries. Pour into greased 9 x 5 x 3-inch loaf pan. Spread corners and sides slightly higher than center. Bake in preheated 350° oven about 1 hour, until golden brown. Cool in pan 10 minutes; remove.

Bread Stuffing

Makes 15 cups

1½ cups finely chopped celery
1 cup chopped onion
½ cup unsalted butter
Dried sage to taste
12 cups dry bread cubes
1 to 1½ cups chicken stock *or* water
Salt and freshly ground black pepper to taste

Sauté celery and onion in butter until tender. Mix in sage to taste. Place bread cubes in large mixing bowl; pour onion mixture over cubes. Add enough stock to moisten bread; toss lightly. Season with salt and pepper. Stuff a 15-pound turkey, or bake in greased casserole at 350° for 30 to 40 minutes, until crusty.

Potato Stuffing

Makes 12 cups

½ cup unsalted butter
2 cups chopped onion
2 cups chopped celery
4 cups bread cubes
1 tablespoon chopped fresh
  parsley
¼ teaspoon freshly ground black
  pepper
4 cups mashed potatoes
1 large egg, lightly beaten
5 tablespoons water

Melt 3 tablespoons butter in a large skillet; sauté onions and celery until soft; set aside. Add remaining butter to another skillet; brown bread cubes over low heat, stirring occasionally. Mix sautéed onions and celery, browned bread cubes, parsley and pepper. Whip potatoes with egg and water; stir in bread mixture and mix thoroughly. Lightly fill body and neck cavities of 12 to 14-pound turkey or bake in greased casserole 30 minutes at 350°.

Brown Rice Stuffing

Makes approximately 3 cups

1 cup brown rice
2½ cups chicken stock
1 teaspoon salt
1 cup chopped onion
1 cup chopped celery
1 clove garlic, crushed
1½ tablespoons unsalted butter
1 teaspoon seasoned salt
  Dash freshly ground black
  pepper
1 cup chopped nuts

Combine rice, stock, and salt in 3-quart saucepan. Heat to boiling; stir. Reduce heat. Cover and simmer 45 minutes. Sauté onion, celery and garlic in butter until tender; stir into cooked rice. Add seasoned salt, pepper and nuts; toss.

Oyster Turkey Stuffing

Makes 4 cups

1 cup unsalted butter
1 cup chopped onion
2 cups fresh bread cubes
½ teaspoon dried thyme, crushed
1 tablespoon chopped fresh
  parsley
  Salt and freshly ground black
  pepper to taste
2 celery stalks, chopped
12 fresh oysters
2 large eggs, lightly beaten
1 cup cracker crumbs
¼ cup unsalted butter

Melt butter in saucepan. Sauté onions until tender. Add bread cubes, thyme, parsley, salt and pepper; stir to combine. Cool and stir in celery; set aside. Roll each oyster in egg, then in cracker crumbs. Heat butter in small skillet; sauté oysters in hot butter 1 minute on each side; set aside. Stuff bird with alternate layers of bread mixture and oysters, or layer in greased casserole, ending with bread mixture. Bake in preheated 325° oven 30 minutes.

Wild Rice Stuffing _____

Makes approximately 3 cups

    3 cups chicken stock
    1 bay leaf
    1 cup wild rice
    3 strips bacon, diced
    1 celery stalk, diced
    1 small onion, diced
    1 carrot, diced
   10 fresh medium mushrooms, sliced
    ¼ cup unsalted butter
       Salt and freshly ground black
       pepper to taste
       Pinch poultry seasoning

Bring stock to a boil; add bay leaf and wild rice. Cover and reduce heat; simmer about 30 minutes, until liquid is absorbed. Partially cook bacon in skillet; add celery, onion, carrot and mushrooms; sauté over medium heat 6 to 7 minutes. Add butter and melt; add to rice. Season to taste and discard bay leaf. Stuff chicken or Cornish game hens, or place in greased casserole; bake in preheated 350° oven 30 minutes.

Mexican Corn Bread Stuffing _____

Makes 15 cups

    1 cup chopped celery
   1½ cups chopped onion
    ½ cup unsalted butter
    1 teaspoon dried sage, crumbled
    ½ teaspoon cumin
    6 cups corn bread cubes, dried
    6 cups dry white bread cubes
    1 can (4 ounces) chopped green
       chilies
    ¼ cup chopped cilantro, optional
    1 cup chicken stock *or* water

Sauté celery and onion in butter until tender. Stir in sage and cumin. Combine bread cubes in large mixing bowl; pour onion mixture over bread. Add chilies and cilantro, if desired. Moisten with chicken stock; toss lightly. Stuff a 15-pound turkey, and bake additional stuffing in greased covered casserole alongside turkey, 30 to 40 minutes at 350°.

Pepper Cheese Bread _____

Makes 1 or 2 loaves

    1 package dry yeast
    ¼ cup warm water
    2 tablespoons sugar
   2⅓ cups flour
    1 teaspoon salt
    ¼ teaspoon baking soda
    1 cup sour cream
    1 large egg
    1 cup shredded Cheddar cheese
    1 teaspoon freshly ground black
       pepper

Grease two 1-pound coffee cans or one 3-inch loaf pan; set aside. Combine yeast, water and 1 teaspoon sugar in bowl; set aside. Combine 1⅓ cups flour, remaining sugar, salt, soda, sour cream and egg in large mixing bowl. Add yeast mixture; beat 2 minutes. Stir in remaining flour, cheese and pepper. Dough will be sticky. Divide dough between cans; let rise 50 minutes. (It will not double in volume.) Bake in preheated 350° oven 40 minutes. Immediately remove from cans. Cool before slicing.

Pepper Cheese Bread, this page.

Rice-Pistachio Stuffing

Makes approximately 10 cups

> 6 tablespoons unsalted butter
> 2 onions, finely chopped
> 2½ cups long-grain rice
> 5 to 6 cups chicken stock
> 1 cup raisins
> ½ teaspoon cinnamon
> ½ teaspoon allspice
> ¼ teaspoon freshly grated nutmeg
> Salt and freshly ground black pepper to taste
> 1 cup shelled pistachio nuts

Melt butter in skillet; add onion and sauté until tender, but not brown. Stir in rice; cook, stirring constantly, until grains are translucent, about 3 minutes. Gradually stir in 5 cups stock; add raisins, spices and seasonings. Cover and bring to a boil over high heat. Reduce heat; simmer 20 to 30 minutes, until liquid is absorbed. If rice is not tender; add remaining stock, cover and cook until absorbed. Cool; stir in nuts. Stuff crown roast, pork, or poultry.

Brown and Serve Rolls

Makes 2 dozen

> 1 package dry yeast
> ¾ cup warm water
> ¾ cup warm milk
> ¼ cup sugar
> 2 teaspoons salt
> ½ cup unsalted butter, cut in pieces
> 3 large eggs, lightly beaten
> 5 to 6 cups flour

Dissolve yeast in water. Add milk, sugar, salt, butter and eggs; stir in 3 cups flour. Mix with wooden spoon. Beat in additional flour to make soft dough. Cover and let rise until doubled in volume. Stir down; spoon into 24 greased muffin cups. Cover and let rise again, about 1 hour. Bake in preheated 250° oven 25 minutes. Cool 25 minutes. Remove from pan. Cool thoroughly before wrapping in plastic bag. Refrigerate up to 1 week. To serve, place rolls on greased baking sheet; bake in preheated 400° oven 10 to 15 minutes.

Mincemeat Bread

Makes 1 loaf

2½ cups flour
1½ teaspoons baking powder
½ teaspoon baking soda
½ teaspoon salt
½ cup unsalted butter, softened
¾ cup sugar
2 large eggs
½ cup milk
1⅓ cups ready-to-use mincemeat
½ cup chopped nuts

Preheat oven to 350°. Stir together flour, baking powder, baking soda and salt; set aside. Beat butter and sugar until fluffy in large mixing bowl. Beat in eggs 1 at a time. Add milk alternately with flour mixture on low speed, blending well. Stir in mincemeat and nuts. Turn into greased 9 x 5 x 3-inch loaf pan; bake 60 to 70 minutes, or until wooden pick inserted near center comes out clean. Cool 10 minutes; remove from pan. Cool completely.

Luscious Lemon Bread with Almond-Lemon Glaze

Makes 2 loaves

1 cup unsalted butter
1 cup sugar
4 large eggs
  Grated rind of 2 lemons
1 can (6 ounces) frozen lemonade
  concentrate, thawed
4 cups flour
4 teaspoons baking powder
1 teaspoon salt
2 teaspoons vanilla
1½ cups half-and-half
¾ to 1 cup chopped pecans
  Almond-Lemon Glaze

Cream butter and sugar in large mixing bowl using electric mixer. Add eggs, 1 at a time, beating well after each addition. Add lemon rind and lemonade; beat well. Sift flour, baking powder and salt together and add to batter. Add vanilla, half-and-half, and pecans; blend well. Pour into two greased 9 x 5 x 3-inch loaf pans; bake in preheated 350° oven for 50 minutes. Cool in pan. Remove from pans; drizzle with Almond-Lemon Glaze.

Almond-Lemon Glaze

Makes ¾ cup

1½ cups powdered sugar
¼ cup unsalted butter, melted
1 tablespoon fresh lemon juice
¼ teaspoon almond extract
¼ teaspoon vanilla extract
  Milk, optional

Combine powdered sugar, butter, lemon juice, and extracts. Mix well, adding a little milk to thin if necessary.

Casserole Dill Bread

Makes 8 to 10 servings

1 package dry yeast
¼ cup warm water
1 cup creamed cottage cheese,
  lukewarm
2 tablespoons sugar
1 tablespoon minced onion
1 tablespoon unsalted butter
2 teaspoons dried dill
1 teaspoon salt
¼ teaspoon baking soda
1 large egg, at room temperature
2¼ to 2½ cups sifted flour

Soften yeast in water. Combine cheese, sugar, onion, butter, dill, salt, soda, egg and softened yeast in large mixing bowl. Stir in enough flour to make stiff ball, beating well after each addition of flour. Dough will be sticky. Place in greased bowl and grease top of dough. Cover; let rise in warm place until doubled, 1 to 1¼ hours. Punch down; turn into greased 8-inch round casserole. Let rise again until doubled, about 40 minutes. Bake in preheated 350° oven 40 to 50 minutes, until golden brown. Brush with additional butter and salt while warm, if desired.

Christmas Date Muffins _____

Makes 1 dozen

    1 cup flour
    ½ teaspoon baking powder
    ½ teaspoon baking soda
    ¼ teaspoon salt
    ¼ teaspoon cinnamon
    ¼ teaspoon freshly grated nutmeg
    1 large egg
    ½ cup light brown sugar
    ¾ cup plain yogurt
    ½ cup slivered pitted dates
    ½ cup chopped walnuts

Stir together flour, baking powder, baking soda, salt, cinnamon and nutmeg. Beat together egg, sugar and yogurt until blended; add flour mixture, dates and nuts. Stir until flour is moistened. Fill 12 greased muffin cups two-thirds full. Bake in preheated 350° oven 25 minutes, or until toothpick inserted in center comes out clean. Serve hot.

Pumpkin Sugar Muffins _____

Makes 1 dozen

    1½ cups flour
    ⅓ cup plus 1½ tablespoons sugar
    2 teaspoons baking powder
    ¼ to ½ teaspoon salt
    ½ teaspoon cinnamon
    ¼ teaspoon freshly grated nutmeg
    ½ cup canned pumpkin purée
    ½ cup milk
    1 large egg, lightly beaten
    ¼ cup unsalted butter, melted
      Additional sugar

Combine flour, ⅓ cup sugar, baking powder and spices; set aside. Mix together pumpkin, milk, egg and butter; stir into flour mixture until flour is moistened. Spoon into 12 greased muffin cups. Sprinkle remaining sugar evenly over muffins; bake in preheated 400° oven 20 minutes. Remove from cups to cool.

Poppy Seed Orange Muffins _____

Makes 1 dozen

    1½ cups flour
    1 cup sugar
    ½ cup sour cream
    ½ cup unsalted butter, softened
    1 large egg
    1 tablespoon poppy seed
    ½ teaspoon salt
    ½ teaspoon baking soda
    2 tablespoons grated orange rind
    2 tablespoons fresh orange juice

Preheat oven to 400°. Beat flour, sugar, sour cream, butter, egg, poppy seed, salt, baking soda, orange rind and juice at low speed in large mixing bowl about 1 minute, or until dry ingredients are moistened. Spoon into 12 greased muffin cups. Bake 17 to 22 minutes, or until lightly browned. Remove from pan to cool.

Sugar Plum Muffins, page 45; Christmas Date Muffins, Poppy Seed Orange Muffins, Pumpkin Sugar Muffins, this page.

Desserts

Pumpkin Charlotte

Makes 6 to 8 servings

14 ladyfingers
⅓ cup rum
2 cups gingersnap cookie crumbs
6 large egg yolks
1 cup sugar
2 cups scalded milk
1 tablespoon unflavored gelatin
3 tablespoons cold water
1 can (16 ounces) pumpkin purée
1 teaspoon cinnamon
¼ teaspoon freshly grated nutmeg
¼ teaspoon ginger
3 tablespoons dark rum
1½ cups whipping cream, whipped
¼ cup toasted slivered almonds

Lightly grease 6-cup brioche mold; set aside. Brush both sides of ladyfingers with rum using pastry brush; roll in gingersnap crumbs. Line mold with ladyfingers, curved side out; chill. Beat egg yolks and sugar in large mixing bowl with electric beater until very thick. Add milk in thin stream, beating constantly. Pour into 2-quart saucepan; cook over medium heat, stirring constantly, until mixture thickens and coats back of spoon. *Do not boil.* Remove from heat. Soften gelatin in cold water. Whisk pumpkin, cinnamon, nutmeg, ginger, rum and softened gelatin into warm mixture. Chill until slightly thickened. Fold ¾ of whipped cream into slightly thickened custard; pour into prepared mold. Cover and chill 4 hours or overnight. To unmold, dip mold in hot water a few seconds. Invert serving platter over mold; flip over to unmold. Garnish with remaining whipped cream and almonds.

Christmas Chocolate Mousse

Makes 6 to 8 servings

8 ounces semisweet *or* bittersweet chocolate
¼ cup prepared strong coffee
6 tablespoons unsalted butter, softened
3 large eggs, separated
¼ teaspoon salt
¼ cup sugar
1½ cups whipping cream
4 red candied cherries, cut into thin strips
4 green candied cherries, cut into thin strips

Break chocolate into pieces; place in top of double boiler over hot, not boiling, water. Add coffee; cook until chocolate melts, stirring occasionally. Remove from heat; pour into large mixing bowl; beat in butter and egg yolks. Beat egg whites in clean, dry mixing bowl until foamy. Add salt; beat to soft peaks. Gradually add sugar; beat to shiny peaks. Fold into chocolate mixture. Whip 1 cup whipping cream to soft peaks; fold into chocolate mixture. Pour into serving bowl or individual parfait glasses. Cover and chill several hours. To serve, whip remaining cream to soft peaks. Garnish mousse with whipped cream and candied cherry strips. Serve immediately.

Buche de Noel (Chocolate Log)

Makes 8 to 10 servings

   4 **large eggs, separated**
   ¾ **cup sugar**
   ½ **cup flour**
   ⅓ **cup cocoa**
   ½ **teaspoon baking soda**
   ¼ **teaspoon salt**
   ⅓ **cup water**
   1 **teaspoon vanilla**
   1 **tablespoon sugar**
     Rum Cream Filling
     Chocolate Frosting
     Red and green candied cherries,
     optional
     Holly leaves, optional

Line a 15 x 10 x 1-inch jelly roll pan with foil; grease foil. Beat egg yolks 2 minutes on medium speed. Gradually add ½ cup sugar; continue beating 2 minutes. Combine flour, cocoa, remaining sugar, baking soda and salt; add alternately with water on low speed just until batter is smooth. Add vanilla; set aside.

Beat egg whites until foamy; add 1 tablespoon sugar; beat until eggs form stiff peaks. Gently fold into chocolate mixture; spread evenly in prepared pan. Bake in preheated 375° oven 14 to 16 minutes, or until top springs back when touched lightly. Invert onto *smooth* towel sprinkled with powdered sugar; carefully remove foil. Immediately roll cake in towel starting from narrow end; place on rack to cool completely. To assemble, unroll cake; remove towel. Spread with Rum Cream Filling; reroll and place on serving tray. Frost with Chocolate Frosting creating a barklike texture with fork or spatula. Garnish with candied cherries and holly leaves, if desired. Cover and refrigerate until serving time.

Rum Cream Filling

Makes 1½ cups

   1 **teaspoon unflavored gelatin**
   1 **tablespoon cold water**
   2 **tablespoons boiling water**
   1 **cup whipping cream**
   ¼ **cup powdered sugar**
   2 **tablespoons rum** *or* ½ **teaspoon**
     rum extract

Sprinkle gelatin over cold water in medium bowl; let stand to soften. Add boiling water; stir until gelatin dissolves. Beat cream with powdered sugar until it holds stiff peaks; blend in rum. Gradually add gelatin mixture, beating until blended. Chill 10 to 15 minutes, until filling begins to set.

Chocolate Frosting

Makes approximately 2 cups

   6 **tablespoons unsalted butter,**
     softened
   ½ **cup cocoa**
  2⅔ **cups powdered sugar**
   4 **to 5 tablespoons milk**
   1 **teaspoon vanilla**

Cream butter until softened in large mixing bowl using electric mixer. Add cocoa; blend well. Gradually and alternately add powdered sugar, milk and vanilla; beat to spreading consistency.

Double Chocolate Torte

Makes 8 to 10 servings

4½ ounces unsweetened chocolate
½ cup unsalted butter
3 cups sifted powdered sugar
½ cup milk
2 large egg whites
1 teaspoon vanilla
½ teaspoon baking powder
¼ teaspoon salt
4 large eggs, at room temperature
¾ cup plus 2 tablespoons sugar
½ cup cake flour
1 teaspoon vanilla
3 ounces unsweetened chocolate
¼ teaspoon baking soda
3 tablespoons cold water
    Whipped cream, optional
    Fresh raspberries, optional
    Chocolate leaves, optional

Melt chocolate and butter in top of double boiler over hot, not boiling, water; cool slightly. Add powdered sugar, milk, egg whites and vanilla; mix well. Set in bowl of ice water; beat with electric mixer until frosting is of a spreading consistency. Chill at least 3 hours.

Combine baking powder, salt and eggs in large mixing bowl. Gradually beat in ¾ cup sugar; continue beating until thick. Fold in flour and vanilla; set aside. Melt chocolate in top of double boiler over hot, not boiling, water. Stir in 2 tablespoons sugar, baking soda and cold water; fold into batter until completely blended. Spread in 10 x 15-inch jelly roll pan lined with waxed paper. Bake in preheated 375° oven 18 to 20 minutes. Loosen sides and turn onto clean cloth to remove cake. Peel off waxed paper; cut away crisp edges of cake. Cool completely. Cut cake into 4 rectangles. Split horizontally into 8 thin layers. Stack layers, spreading about ¼ cup of frosting between each layer. Cover top and sides of torte with remaining frosting. Decorate with whipped cream rosettes, fresh raspberries, or chocolate leaves, if desired.

Nutty Cranberry Tarts

Makes 30 tarts

1 package (3 ounces) cream cheese, softened
½ cup unsalted butter, softened
1 cup flour
1 large egg
¾ cup light brown sugar
1 tablespoon unsalted butter
1 teaspoon vanilla
    Dash salt
⅔ cup chopped pecans
¼ cup chopped fresh cranberries

Beat cream cheese, butter and flour in mixing bowl using electric mixer; chill. Divide mixture into 30 balls; press into 1½-inch fluted tart shell tins or miniature muffin tins. Set aside. Beat egg, brown sugar, butter, vanilla and salt in mixing bowl using electric mixer; stir in nuts and cranberries. Spoon into tart shells; bake in preheated 325° oven for 25 minutes.
Note: Tarts can be frozen. Wrap tightly in foil. Thaw in wrappings and serve.

Plum Pudding with Hard Sauce

Makes 8 to 10 servings

½ pound stale bread crumbs
1 cup scalded milk
½ cup plus 2 tablespoons sugar
4 large eggs, separated
¾ pound seedless raisins, lightly floured
¼ pound figs, finely chopped
2 ounces citron, finely chopped
½ pound suet
¼ cup red currant jelly
½ teaspoon freshly grated nutmeg
¾ teaspoon cinnamon
¼ teaspoon cloves
¼ teaspoon mace
1½ teaspoons salt
Hard Sauce

Combine bread crumbs and milk in large mixing bowl; let stand until cool. Add sugar, beaten egg yolks, raisins, figs and citron. Chop suet; beat until creamy. Add to bread; blend. Beat egg whites in a clean, dry mixing bowl until they hold stiff peaks. Add beaten whites, jelly, nutmeg, cinnamon, cloves, mace, and salt to bread.

Butter 8 or 10 pudding molds. Fill ⅔ full; place on trivet in kettle. Add boiling water until it comes up halfway along outside of mold. Keep water at boiling point while steaming. Cover pan and steam 6 hours. Add additional boiling water as needed to maintain level. To unmold, remove from steamer; set in cold water a few seconds, then turn out onto serving platter. If desired, set in oven a few minutes to dry slightly. Serve with Hard Sauce.

Hard Sauce

Makes ¾ cup

⅓ cup unsalted butter
1 cup light brown sugar
2 tablespoons brandy

Cream butter. Gradually add brown sugar and brandy, drop by drop, until smooth.

Orchard Apple Cake

Makes 12 servings

2 cups sugar
1 cup unsalted butter, softened
2 large eggs, lightly beaten
2 cups flour
1 teaspoon baking soda
1 teaspoon salt
1 teaspoon freshly grated nutmeg
2 teaspoons cinnamon
Juice and grated rind of 1 lemon
5 cups finely chopped Jonathan apples
1 cup chopped walnuts
1 cup whipping cream, whipped, optional

Cream sugar and butter in large mixing bowl until fluffy. Beat in eggs. Sift dry ingredients into another bowl. Add to creamed ingredients; mix just until blended. Beat in lemon juice and rind; fold in apples and nuts; pour into greased 9 x 13-inch baking pan. Bake in preheated 350° oven 1 hour; cool. To serve, cut into squares, and garnish with whipped cream, if desired. Serve immediately.

Old-Fashioned Fruitcake _____

Makes two 10-inch cakes

2 pounds raisins
2 pounds currants
½ pound candied citron
1 pound candied cherries, reserve some for garnish
1 pound candied yellow, red and green pineapple, reserve some for garnish
¼ pound candied lemon peel
¼ pound candied orange peel
12 ounces grated coconut
½ pound walnuts, chopped
½ cup chopped pecans, reserve 6 whole pecans
1¼ cups flour
1 teaspoon allspice
1 teaspoon cloves
1 teaspoon freshly grated nutmeg
1 teaspoon cinnamon
¾ teaspoon salt
1 pound unsalted butter
1¼ cups sugar
12 large eggs
1 cup apple juice

Grease and flour two 10-inch tube pans. Place waxed paper on bottom of pans; set aside. Combine raisins, currants, citron, cherries, pineapple, lemon peel, orange peel, coconut, walnuts and pecans in very large mixing bowl. Mix flour and spices; gradually blend into fruit, coating well. Cream butter and sugar until light and fluffy. Beat in eggs 1 at a time. Beat in apple juice. Combine with fruit and flour mixture until blended well. Pour into pans. Garnish with ½ slice each candied yellow, red and green pineapple and 3 candied red cherry halves. Place 2 pecan halves between pineapple slices.

Preheat oven to 225°; place broiler pan with water on bottom rack of oven. Put cakes on low rack right above water. Bake 4 to 4½ hours, or until toothpick inserted in cakes comes out clean. Cool in pans; invert onto rack. Wrap tightly in plastic and foil until serving time.

Pear Rum Trifle _____

Makes 8 servings

3 large egg yolks
¾ cup sugar
2 teaspoons grated lemon rind
2 cups milk
2 tablespoons rum
1 pound cake
¼ cup rum
2 tablespoons fresh lemon juice
4 ripe Bartlett pears, chopped
½ cup whipping cream, whipped

Beat egg yolks, ¼ cup sugar and lemon rind in top of double boiler over hot, not boiling, water. Gradually blend in milk; cook, stirring until slightly thickened. Remove from heat; add 2 tablespoons rum; cool. Cut pound cake into ½-inch thick slices; spoon a little rum on each. Arrange ⅔ of slices over bottom and around sides of a round 2-quart dish. Combine remaining ½ cup sugar and lemon juice in 1-quart saucepan. Add pears. Stir over medium heat 5 to 8 minutes, mashing slightly; spoon over cake. Top with remaining cake slices; pour cooled custard over all. Cover and chill 6 hours or overnight. To serve, cut into wedges and garnish each serving with whipped cream.

Brandied Mincemeat Chiffon Pie

Makes 6 to 8 servings

½ cup brandy
1 cup mincemeat
1 envelope unflavored gelatin
1 tablespoon fresh lemon juice
¼ cup sugar
¼ teaspoon salt
1 teaspoon grated fresh lemon rind
⅔ cup milk
3 large eggs, separated
1 cup whipping cream
1 baked 9-inch pie crust with high fluted rim

Combine brandy, mincemeat, gelatin and lemon juice in small saucepan; let stand 5 minutes. Heat slowly, stirring occasionally, until gelatin dissolves. Combine 2 tablespoons sugar, salt, rind, milk and lightly beaten egg yolks in top of double boiler over hot, not boiling, water. Cook, stirring constantly, until slightly thickened, about 5 minutes. Remove from heat. Stir in mincemeat mixture; cool until mixture begins to thicken and jell. Beat egg whites in clean, dry mixing bowl until frothy. Beat in remaining sugar, a tablespoon at a time. Whip cream to soft peaks. Fold egg whites and cream into pie filling. Chill 15 minutes; turn into pie crust. Chill until firm, at least 5 hours.

White Fruitcake

Makes 7 mini loaves

1 pound unsalted butter, at room temperature
2 cups sugar
6 large eggs, at room temperature
4 cups flour
5 teaspoons baking powder
1 bottle (2 ounces) lemon extract
1 pound chopped nuts
1 pound candied cherries
1 pound candied pineapple

Cream butter and sugar until fluffy. Add eggs, 1 at a time, beating well after each addition. Sift flour with baking powder; add to butter alternately with lemon extract using low speed of electric mixer. Pour over chopped nuts and fruit in large bowl; blend. Pour into 7 miniature well-greased and floured loaf pans; bake in preheated 275° oven 1¾ to 2 hours. Cool in pans. Remove from pans; wrap in airtight wrap. Store in cool place 2 weeks before slicing.

Pecan Pie

Makes 6 to 8 servings

3 large eggs, lightly beaten
1 cup sugar
1 cup light *or* dark corn syrup
1 tablespoon unsalted butter, melted
1 teaspoon vanilla
1 cup whole pecans
1 unbaked 9-inch pie crust

Stir eggs, sugar, corn syrup, butter and vanilla together in large mixing bowl until blended. Stir in pecans. Pour into pie crust. Bake in preheated 350° oven for 50 to 60 minutes, or until knife inserted halfway between center and edge of pie comes out clean. Cool.

Nutty Cranberry Tarts, page 59; Pumpkin Ice Cream in a Gingersnap Crust, page 64; Pecan Pie, Brandied Mincemeat Chiffon Pie, this page.

Pumpkin Ice Cream in a Gingersnap Crust

Makes approximately 6 servings

1 cup canned cooked pumpkin
  purée
¼ cup sugar
1½ teaspoons pumpkin pie spice
1 pint vanilla ice cream, softened
2 tablespoons fresh lemon juice
1 cup whipping cream, whipped
  Gingersnap Crumb Crust
  Pecan halves, optional

Combine pumpkin, sugar and spice in mixing bowl. Spoon in softened ice cream; blend. Fold in lemon juice and whipped cream; blend well. Freeze, if necessary, until mixture begins to set. Spoon into Gingersnap Crumb Crust; freeze until firm, at least 4 hours or overnight. Garnish with pecan halves, if desired. Store in freezer.

Gingersnap Crumb Crust

Makes one 9-inch pie crust

1¼ cups gingersnap crumbs
¼ cup sugar
¼ cup unsalted butter, melted

Combine crumbs, sugar and butter in small mixing bowl; mix well. Press firmly on bottom and sides of 9-inch pie pan. Bake in preheated oven 8 minutes. Cool.

Cranberry Pudding with Cream Sauce

Makes 9 servings

2 teaspoons baking soda
⅓ cup hot water
1½ cups flour
2 tablespoons sugar
½ cup light molasses
½ teaspoon salt
2 cups fresh whole cranberries
  Cream Sauce

Combine baking soda and water in large mixing bowl. Stir in flour, sugar, molasses and salt. Add cranberries; mix well. Pour into greased and floured 9 x 9-inch baking pan. Bake in preheated 300° oven for 35 minutes, or until toothpick inserted in center comes out clean. Pour hot Cream Sauce over pudding; serve immediately.

Cream Sauce

Makes 1 cup

½ cup unsalted butter
1 cup sugar
½ cup whipping cream

Melt butter in 1-quart saucepan. Add sugar and cream; bring to a boil. Serve over hot Cranberry Pudding.

Date Pudding and Brown Sugar Topping

Makes 8 servings

1 cup flour
1 cup sugar
2 teaspoons baking powder
1 cup chopped dates
1 cup chopped pecans
½ cup milk
  Brown Sugar Topping
  Whipped cream

Combine flour, sugar, baking powder, dates, pecans and milk in large mixing bowl; mix well. Pour into greased 9-inch square baking pan. Pour Brown Sugar Topping over batter. Bake in preheated 350° oven for 1 hour. Serve with whipped cream.

Brown Sugar Topping

Makes 2 cups

2 cups boiling water
1 cup light brown sugar, packed
1 tablespoon unsalted butter

Combine boiling water, brown sugar and butter; mix well. Use as directed in Date Pudding recipe.

Frost on the Pumpkin Torte

Makes 12 servings

1 cup flour
½ cup unsalted butter, softened
½ cup finely chopped walnuts
2 packages (8 ounces each) cream cheese, at room temperature
⅔ cup sugar
3 large eggs, separated
1 teaspoon vanilla
2 envelopes unflavored gelatin
¾ cup cold milk
2 cups cooked pumpkin purée
¾ cup light brown sugar
½ teaspoon cinnamon
1 teaspoon pumpkin pie spice
1 teaspoon vanilla
½ cup powdered sugar
  Whipped cream, optional

Mix flour, butter and walnuts; press into a 9 x 13-inch baking pan; set aside. Blend cream cheese, sugar, beaten egg yolks and vanilla; pour over crust. Bake in preheated 350° oven for 15 to 20 minutes; cool. Soften gelatin in milk; combine with pumpkin, sugar, cinnamon, pumpkin pie spice and vanilla in 2-quart saucepan. Cook about 5 minutes; cool. Beat egg whites in clean, dry bowl until frothy. Gradually beat in powdered sugar until eggs form stiff peaks. Fold into pumpkin mixture; pour over cream cheese layer. Individual servings can be topped with whipped cream, if desired.

Holiday Pumpkin Cake Roll with Cheese Filling

Makes 8 to 10 servings

3 large eggs
1 cup sugar
⅔ cup cooked pumpkin purée
1 teaspoon fresh lemon juice
¾ cup flour
1 teaspoon baking powder
2 teaspoons cinnamon
1 teaspoon ginger
½ teaspoon salt
½ teaspoon freshly grated nutmeg
1 cup finely chopped pecans
Powdered sugar
Cheese Filling
Whipped cream, optional

Beat eggs, sugar, pumpkin and lemon juice in large bowl of electric mixer 5 minutes. Sift flour, baking powder, cinnamon, ginger, salt and nutmeg into another bowl. Fold pumpkin mixture into dry ingredients; pour into greased and floured 10 x 15-inch jelly roll pan. Sprinkle with nuts; bake in preheated 375° oven for 15 minutes. Turn out onto smooth towel, sprinkled with powdered sugar. Roll up starting at narrow end; cool. Unroll and spread with Cheese Filling; reroll. Wrap in foil and chill until serving time. Unwrap and transfer to serving platter; decorate with whipped cream, if desired.

Cheese Filling

Makes 1½ cups

2 packages (3 ounces each) cream cheese, softened
1 cup powdered sugar
¼ cup unsalted butter, softened
1 teaspoon vanilla

Combine all filling ingredients in mixing bowl; beat until fluffy. Spread on Pumpkin Cake as directed.

Thanksgiving Pumpkin Pie

Makes 6 to 8 servings

2 large eggs, lightly beaten
2 cups cooked pumpkin purée
¾ cup sugar
½ teaspoon salt
1 teaspoon cinnamon
½ teaspoon ginger
¼ teaspoon cloves
1 teaspoon vanilla
1 teaspoon maple flavoring, optional
1 can (13 ounces) evaporated milk
1 9-inch unbaked pie crust with high fluted rim
Whipped cream, optional

Combine eggs, pumpkin, sugar, salt, spices, flavorings and milk in large mixing bowl; beat to mix well. Pour into pie crust; bake in preheated 425° oven for 15 minutes. Reduce temperature to 350°; bake another 45 minutes, until filling is set. Cool on rack. Garnish with whipped cream, if desired.

Holiday Pumpkin Cake Roll with Cheese Filling, this page.

Gifts

Apricot Florentines

Makes 4 dozen

- ½ cup minced dried apricots
- 2 tablespoons minced candied ginger
- ¾ cup chopped pecans
- 1 cup flour
- 1 teaspoon grated orange rind
- 6 tablespoons unsalted butter, softened
- ½ cup sugar
- 2 tablespoons honey
- 2 tablespoons whipping cream
- 2 tablespoons rum
- 8 ounces semisweet chocolate chips

Mix apricots, ginger, pecans, flour and orange rind in large mixing bowl; set aside. Heat butter, sugar, honey, cream and rum in heavy saucepan, stirring occasionally until sugar dissolves. Remove from heat. Combine with dry ingredients in mixing bowl. Drop by teaspoonfuls on greased baking sheet; flatten with back of spoon into very thin circles. Bake in preheated 350° oven until light brown. Remove from baking sheet immediately; cool. Melt chocolate in top of double boiler set over hot, not boiling, water. Spread cookies with melted chocolate; let set until hard.

Brandy Creme

Makes approximately 2 quarts

- 6 large egg yolks
- ¾ cup sugar
- 1 can (15 ounces) sweetened condensed milk
- 2½ cups brandy
- ½ cup water
- 1 whole vanilla bean

Beat egg yolks and sugar in mixing bowl until thick; stir in sweetened condensed milk, brandy and water. Strain several times, until no sediment remains. Pour into 2-quart glass container. Add vanilla bean and cover tightly. Allow to age in cool, dark place 3 months, or up to 1 year. Shake mixture weekly during first month, until there is no separation. Remove vanilla bean; pour into decanters and cap tightly. Liqueur will keep 5 months in refrigerator after opening.

Secret Kiss Cookies

Makes 4 dozen

- 1 cup unsalted butter, at room temperature
- ½ cup sugar
- 1 teaspoon vanilla
- 2 cups flour
- 1 cup ground walnuts
- 1 package (9 ounces) chocolate kisses, unwrapped
  Powdered sugar, optional

Cream butter and sugar in large mixing bowl until fluffy. Add vanilla, flour and nuts; mix by hand to combine. Wrap each chocolate kiss completely with 1 teaspoon dough. Place on greased baking sheet; bake in preheated 350° oven about 10 minutes, until light brown. While still warm, roll in powdered sugar, if desired.

68

Chocolate Creme Cups

Makes 2 dozen

1½ cups flour
1 teaspoon baking soda
1 cup sugar
¼ cup cocoa
½ teaspoon salt
1 cup water
⅓ cup vegetable oil
1 tablespoon vinegar
1 teaspoon vanilla
   Chocolate Cream Filling
   Additional sugar

Sift flour, baking soda, sugar, cocoa and salt into large mixing bowl. Stir in water, oil, vinegar and vanilla; mix thoroughly. Fill 24 cupcake liners ⅓ full. Top with 1 heaping tablespoon of Chocolate Cream Filling. Sprinkle with sugar. Bake in preheated 325° oven for 25 minutes.

Chocolate Cream Filling

Makes 2½ cups

1 package (8 ounces) cream cheese, softened
1 large egg
⅓ cup sugar
⅛ teaspoon salt
1 cup semisweet chocolate chips
½ cup chopped pecans

Beat cream cheese, egg, sugar and salt until mixed. Stir in chocolate chips and nuts. Use as directed in Chocolate Creme Cups.

Individual Fruitcakes

Makes approximately 4 dozen

1 cup vegetable oil
1½ cups light brown sugar
4 large eggs
3 cups flour
1 teaspoon baking powder
2 teaspoons salt
2 teaspoons cinnamon
2 teaspoons allspice
1 teaspoon cloves
1 cup fresh orange juice
⅓ cup brandy
1 package (8 ounces) candied fruit
1 package (4 ounces) candied pineapple
1 package (4 ounces) candied cherries
2 cups chopped dates
2 cups chopped pecans

Beat oil and sugar in large mixing bowl until combined. Add eggs; beat until light. Sift flour, baking powder, salt, cinnamon, allspice and cloves together; reserve 1 cup. Add alternately with orange juice and brandy to egg mixture. Mix reserved dry ingredients with candied fruits. Stir dates, pecans and fruit mixture into batter. Completely fill cupcake liners. Bake in preheated 325° oven 25 minutes or until toothpick inserted in fruitcakes comes out clean.

Tassies

Makes 4 dozen

2 cups sifted flour
2 packages (3 ounces each) cream cheese, softened
1 cup unsalted butter, softened
Pecan Filling

Combine flour, cream cheese and butter; mix. Wrap in plastic and chill. Shape into walnut-sized balls. Press into miniature muffin cups, 1¾ inches in diameter. Drop about 1 teaspoon Pecan Filling into each pastry shell. Bake in preheated 350° oven for 25 minutes. Cool. Store in refrigerator.

Pecan Filling

Makes approximately 2 cups

3 tablespoons unsalted butter
3 large eggs, lightly beaten
2 cups light brown sugar
1 cup chopped pecans
1 teaspoon vanilla
¼ teaspoon salt

Melt butter in 1-quart saucepan. Add eggs, brown sugar, pecans, vanilla and salt; cook about 5 minutes, stirring constantly. Use as directed for Tassies.

Lemon Supremes

Makes approximately 5 dozen

½ cup unsalted butter
1 cup plus 1 tablespoon flour
¼ cup powdered sugar
2 tablespoons fresh lemon juice
Grated rind of 1 lemon
2 large eggs, lightly beaten
½ teaspoon baking powder
1 cup sugar

Preheat oven to 350°. Blend butter, 1 cup flour and powdered sugar in large bowl; mix well. Press into 9-inch square baking pan. Bake 15 minutes. Whisk together lemon juice, rind, eggs, baking powder, remaining flour and sugar. Pour over crust; bake 25 minutes. Cool in pan. Cut into squares; place in paper holders.

Candied Pecans

Makes 4 cups

4 cups pecans
½ cup sugar
½ teaspoon cinnamon
¼ teaspoon ginger
¼ teaspoon freshly grated nutmeg
¼ teaspoon allspice
Oil
Salt, optional

Cover pecans with water in saucepan; bring to a boil. Boil 1 minute and drain well. Mix sugar and spices; set aside. While pecans are still warm, toss with sugar mixture. Spread on tray in single layer; let dry, 8 to 24 hours. Heat oil to 350°. Fry nuts about 2 minutes, until sugar caramelizes and nuts are dark brown. Drain well. Sprinkle with salt while still warm, if desired. Store in airtight container.

Hot Spiced Tea, page 13; Individual Fruitcakes, page 69; Tassies,
Lemon Supremes, this page.

Rum Cherries

Makes approximately 3½ quarts

2 cups sugar
1 cup water
6 cups maraschino cherries
2 cups vodka
2 cups light rum
2 whole cinnamon sticks

Combine sugar and water in heavy 1-quart saucepan over medium heat. Bring to a boil; boil 2 minutes. Cool and transfer to 4-quart glass container. Add cherries, vodka, rum and cinnamon sticks; cover. Let stand in cool, dark place 6 weeks, shaking occasionally. Strain to remove sediment. Serve cherries and liquid separately, or combine in gift decanters.

Peppermint Pinwheels

Makes 6 to 8 dozen

1 cup unsalted butter, at room temperature
1 cup powdered sugar
1 large egg
1½ teaspoons peppermint extract
1 teaspoon vanilla extract
2¾ cups flour
½ teaspoon salt
Red or green food coloring
½ cup powdered sugar

Cream butter and powdered sugar. Mix in egg and extracts. Add flour and salt; blend thoroughly. Cover and chill overnight. Divide dough; add food coloring to one portion. Roll plain dough on waxed paper dusted with powdered sugar to ½-inch thickness. Repeat with colored dough; place over other. Remove waxed paper; gently roll into log. Chill 2 hours. Cut in ¼-inch slices and place on ungreased baking sheets. Bake in preheated 375° oven 10 minutes.

Turtle Squares

Makes approximately 10 dozen

2 cups flour
1¾ cups light or dark brown sugar
1½ cups unsalted butter
1 cup pecan halves
1 cup semisweet chocolate chips

Combine flour, 1 cup brown sugar, and ½ cup softened butter in large mixing bowl; blend until smooth. Press into 9 x 13-inch baking pan. Arrange pecans evenly over crust; set aside. Melt remaining butter and remaining sugar in heavy saucepan over low heat. Increase heat; bring to a full boil. Immediately remove from heat; do not overcook. Pour over pecans. Bake in preheated 350° oven 20 minutes, or until top is bubbly and crust is golden. Remove from oven; sprinkle with chocolate chips. To create marbling, swirl chocolate as it melts. Cool completely in pan before cutting into squares.

Almond Delights

Makes 6 to 7 dozen

2 large eggs
½ cup sugar
½ teaspoon cinnamon
½ teaspoon cloves
   Pinch freshly grated nutmeg
4 drops lemon extract
4 drops rum extract
2 drops almond extract
1 cup ground almonds
1¼ cups chopped almonds
¾ cup finely chopped citron
1½ cups powdered sugar
2 to 3 tablespoons hot water
   Colored sugar

Beat eggs and sugar in large mixing bowl. Add spices and extracts; mix well. Fold in almonds and citron. Drop teaspoonfuls onto greased baking sheets. Bake in preheated 350° oven for 20 minutes. Blend powdered sugar and water together to form thick paste. Spread on warm cookies; sprinkle with colored sugar.

Chocolate Caramel Bars

Makes approximately 5 dozen

7 tablespoons unsalted butter
1 package (6 ounces) chocolate chips
1 package (10 ounces) caramels, unwrapped
2 tablespoons water
1 cup coarsely chopped nuts

Melt 2 tablespoons butter and chocolate in top of double boiler over hot, not boiling, water. Spread half of mixture into 8-inch foil-lined baking pan; chill 15 minutes. Melt caramels, water and remaining butter in saucepan; stir until smooth. Stir in nuts. Spread over chilled chocolate layer; chill another 15 minutes. Remelt remaining chocolate mixture, if necessary; spread over caramel layer. Chill 1 hour before cutting into bars.

Peanut Brittle

Makes approximately 1 pound

2 cups sugar
1 cup light corn syrup
½ cup water
1 cup unsalted butter
2½ cups dry roasted peanuts
1 teaspoon baking soda
1 teaspoon vanilla

Combine sugar, corn syrup and water in heavy 3-quart saucepan over medium heat; stir until sugar dissolves. When syrup boils, add butter. Cook, stirring frequently, until candy thermometer registers 280°. Immediately add peanuts; stir constantly, until temperature reaches 305°. Remove from heat. Add baking soda and vanilla; mix well. Immediately spread onto 2 baking sheets. Cool and break into bite-sized pieces.

Amaretti

Makes 3 dozen

    8 ounces almond paste
    2 large egg whites
      Pinch salt
    1 teaspoon vanilla
    1 cup sifted powdered sugar

Grease and flour 2 large baking sheets; set aside. Break up almond paste in medium mixing bowl. Add egg whites, salt and vanilla; beat on low speed until mixture is smooth. Slowly add powdered sugar, beating at low speed until soft dough forms. Drop teaspoonfuls onto prepared baking sheets. Bake in preheated 325° oven about 20 minutes, until light golden brown. Let stand 1 minute on baking sheets; remove to cool. Store in airtight container.

Note: Cookies should be chewy, not crisp.

Exquisite Truffles

Makes approximately 2 dozen

    8 ounces bittersweet chocolate
    ¼ cup plus 2 tablespoons unsalted
      butter
    3 large egg yolks
    1 teaspoon vanilla
      Unsweetened cocoa

Melt chocolate and butter in top of double boiler over hot, not boiling, water. Beat egg yolks in small bowl; gradually beat into melted chocolate. Add vanilla and cool until firm enough to hold shape. Dust hands with cocoa; form chocolate into irregular shaped balls about size of walnut. Dust with more cocoa. Arrange truffles in fluted paper candy cups or on doily. Cover and refrigerate until serving time.

Mocha Fudge

Makes approximately 6 dozen

    ½ cup powdered sugar
    ¾ cup cocoa
    1 cup finely chopped nuts
    ¾ cup unsalted butter, softened
    ¾ cup evaporated milk
    2 tablespoons instant coffee
      granules
    1 jar (17 ounces) marshmallow
      creme
    ½ cup unsalted butter, cold

Sift powdered sugar and cocoa into a heatproof bowl. Stir in nuts; set aside. Melt softened butter in heavy saucepan. Stir in milk and coffee granules. Bring to a rolling boil over medium heat, stirring constantly, until candy thermometer registers 234°. Remove from heat; pour over cocoa mixture. Stir with wooden spoon until completely blended. Add marshmallow creme and cold butter; blend well. Turn into greased 9 x 13-inch pan. Cool completely and cut into squares.

Exquisite Truffles, Mocha Fudge, this page.

Toffee Brittle

Makes 1¼ pounds

1⅔ cups sugar
⅔ cup dark corn syrup
⅓ cup half-and-half
¼ cup unsalted butter
⅓ cup coarsely chopped nuts
½ teaspoon vanilla

Grease an 8-inch square baking pan; set aside. Combine sugar, corn syrup and half-and-half in heavy 3-quart saucepan; cook over medium heat, stirring constantly, until mixture boils. Add butter; cook over low heat, stirring occasionally, until candy thermometer registers 280°. Remove from heat; stir in nuts and vanilla. Continue stirring 2 minutes. Turn into prepared pan; cool slightly. Use a sharp knife to mark candy into ½-inch squares. Press along marks with a flat metal spatula. Repeat, pressing deeper each time, until spatula reaches bottom of pan and candy is shaped into puffs. Cool completely. Turn out onto a board and break into pieces.

Nutmeg Bars

Makes 8 dozen

1 cup unsalted butter, softened (do not use margarine)
1 cup sugar
1 large egg, separated
2 cups sifted flour
1½ teaspoons freshly grated nutmeg

Cream butter and sugar in large mixing bowl until fluffy. Add egg yolk; beat well. Stir in flour and nutmeg. Spread in an 11 x 17-inch ungreased jelly roll pan. Slightly beat egg white; brush over dough. Smooth surface with fingertips. Bake in preheated 275° oven, about 1 hour, until rich golden brown. While hot, cut into rectangular bars.
Note: If a shiny jelly roll pan is used, baking time will be longer, about 1¼ hours.

Sugar Plums

Makes approximately 3 dozen

¼ cup dried apricots, finely chopped
¼ cup dried figs, finely chopped
¼ cup golden raisins, finely chopped
½ cup chopped pecans
¼ cup grated coconut
2 tablespoons orange liqueur
¼ cup sugar

Blend chopped ingredients together; moisten with orange liqueur. Firmly shape into 1-inch balls. Roll in sugar. Layer between waxed paper in an airtight container. Store in refrigerator. Sugar plums will keep up to 1 month.
Note: Using a melon baller to form balls speeds procedure.

Almond Butter Cookies

Makes approximately 6 dozen

1½ **cups sugar**
1 **cup unsalted butter, softened**
1 **package (8 ounces) cream cheese, softened**
1 **large egg**
½ **teaspoon vanilla extract**
1 **teaspoon almond extract**
1 **teaspoon baking powder**
3½ **cups flour**

Cream sugar, butter and cheese in large mixing bowl until light. Beat in egg and extracts. Combine baking powder and flour; slowly add to butter mixture. Refrigerate.

Roll out on floured surface; cut out with cookie cutters; place on lightly greased baking sheets; bake in preheated 375° oven 8 to 10 minutes. Cool. Frost and decorate as desired.

Note: This is a very basic dough; many different cookies can be made from it. Put dough through cookie press and bake as described above. For pinwheel cookies, divide dough. Add food coloring or 1 ounce melted chocolate to one half; mix well. Refrigerate dough 30 minutes. Roll out both halves. Place one on top of the other; roll up. Refrigerate 30 minutes; slice and bake as directed. Dough also can be used for drop cookies. Top with 1 cherry or nut before baking as directed above.

Amaretto Chocolate Sauce

Makes approximately 1 cup

8 **ounces semisweet** *or* **bittersweet chocolate, broken into pieces**
1 **tablespoon unsalted butter**
1 **teaspoon amaretto liqueur**

Melt chocolate and butter in top of double boiler set over hot, not boiling, water. Remove from heat; stir in liqueur. Serve hot over ice cream.

Spicy Holiday Aroma

Makes approximately ½ cup

2 **tablespoons cinnamon**
1 **tablespoon allspice**
1 **tablespoon plus 2 teaspoons cloves**
2 **teaspoons grated orange rind**
1 **teaspoon grated lemon rind**

Combine cinnamon, allspice, cloves, orange and lemon rinds. Sprinkle 2 tablespoons of this mixture over 3 cups boiling water. Reduce heat; simmer for spicy aroma. Additional water can be added as it evaporates.

Best-Ever Christmas Cookies

Makes 2½ dozen

1¼ **cups almonds**
1¼ **cups sugar**
2½ **cups flour**
   1 **teaspoon vanilla**
   6 **large egg yolks, chilled**
   1 **cup unsalted butter, slightly softened**
   1 **jar (8 ounces) red currant, strawberry** *or* **raspberry jelly**
     Powdered sugar

Combine almonds with ½ cup sugar in work bowl of food processor fitted with steel blade. Process until fine. Add remaining sugar and flour. Blend until fine, 25 to 30 seconds. Place on dry, cold marble or countertop. Make a well in center; add vanilla, egg yolks and butter. Slowly work together until moisture is absorbed. Knead until mixture is completely smooth, 3 to 4 minutes. Refrigerate 4 to 6 hours.

Divide dough; cover and refrigerate. Roll one portion of dough on cold floured surface to ¼-inch thickness. Cut rounds with 1½ to 2-inch fluted cookie cutter. Place on baking sheets lined with parchment paper. Cut ½-inch circles out of centers.

Bake in preheated 350° oven for 10 to 12 minutes, until slightly browned around edges. Carefully remove from baking sheet; cool. Repeat with second portion of dough, *but do not cut out centers.* To assemble cookies, spread thin layer of jelly on each of whole cookies. Top with cut-out cookies. If desired, fill holes with extra jelly using a pastry bag. Sprinkle with powdered sugar.

Note: Bake cut-out cookie centers for snacks.

Chocolate Dipped Creams

Makes 6 dozen

   1 **cup flour**
   1 **cup cornstarch**
   1 **cup unsalted butter, softened**
   ½ **cup powdered sugar**
   ⅛ **teaspoon salt**
   1 **teaspoon vanilla**
     Powdered sugar
     Melted semisweet *or* **bittersweet chocolate**
     Chopped nuts
     Flaked coconut
     Assorted jimmies

Sift flour and cornstarch; set aside. Cream butter in large mixing bowl. Gradually add powdered sugar; cream well. Add salt, vanilla and sifted ingredients. Chill 2 or 3 hours. Shape into small rounds, triangles, crescents, and bars. Place 2 inches apart on greased baking sheet. Bake in preheated 350° oven 15 to 20 minutes. While hot, roll in powdered sugar. Dip cookies in melted chocolate; then dip in chopped nuts, coconut or jimmies. Allow chocolate to harden before storing.

Peppermint Pinwheels, page 72; Chocolate Dipped Creams, Best-Ever Christmas Cookies, this page.